Learning Works

Widening Participation in Further Education

Helena
Kennedy QC

Contents

Learning Works

Main report of the Widening Participation Committee

One of the aims of the Further Education Funding Council is to promote access to further education for people who do not participate in education and training, but who could benefit from it. The Council set up the widening participation committee in December 1994 to advise it on achieving that aim. The committee was chaired by Helena Kennedy QC. The terms of reference of the committee are set out in annex A. Evidence given to the committee is summarised in annex B. The membership of the committee is given in annex C.

The committee's emerging conclusions were published in *Pathways to Success* in February 1997. A consultation document setting out its proposals for strategic partnerships and the 'New Learning Pathway' was published in March 1997. *Identifying and Addressing Needs – A practical guide*, commissioned jointly by the widening participation committee and the committee on learning difficulties and/or disabilities chaired by Professor John Tomlinson, was published in March 1997.

Two companion volumes to Learning Works: a good practice guide for institutions based on the research undertaken on behalf of the committee by the Council's inspectorate; and the committee's statistical evidence, including a framework for institutions to measure participation, will be published in September. Some key contributions to the committee's evidence base will also be published. Dissemination of the committee's work and consultation on its recommendations will take place in the autumn.

doughty street chambers

11 Doughty Street
London WC1N 2PG

Dear Sir Robert,

I am delighted to present the report of the widening participation committee to the Council. On behalf of the committee, I would like to thank you and the Council for entrusting us with such a vital task. In the report we set out an agenda for change to increase access to post-16 learning and to improve the quality of learners' achievements. The issues we have considered reflect closely those which are at the heart of the government's education agenda. We now look to both government and the Council to implement our recommendations as part of a concerted national effort to widen participation.

To thank all those individuals and organisations from whom I have received support and inspiration during the last two years would fill another volume. The members of the committee were the bedrock of the endeavour. Each one has brought rich perspectives and expertise to bear on the work. Out of common commitment and diversity of individual views and experience, we discovered a shared approach to values, and agreement about the need for action.

The staff, governors, and students in colleges and other organisations we have visited, fired our imaginations. Seeing wonderful examples of the ways in which learning opportunities have been extended to more and different kinds of learners and talking to the learners, reinforced our determination to produce a report which would have a real impact on people's lives.

Many distinguished and eminent people found space in their diaries for the three seminars we organised to test some of our early conclusions and ideas. Their wisdom and insight proved invaluable. We hope we have done justice to their contributions.

The volume and quality of responses to our requests for oral and written evidence were testimony to the widespread interest in our work. *Pathways to Success* and the consultation document also produced healthy and thought-provoking postbags. Many people from all walks of life wrote to me personally with their ideas and wished me well. To all of them a special thank you.

Our work has been strengthened by some significant external contributions. The survey of the issues by Hilary Steedman, of the Centre for Economic Performance, and Andy Green, of the Institute of Education, got us off to an excellent start. Claire Callender and Alicia Herbert, of the Policy Studies Institute, gathered together the key sources on student financial support. Caroline Mager, and her team from the Further Education Development Agency, provided us with much food for thought and some practical ideas on credit frameworks. Alan Tuckett and Naomi Sargant, of the National Institute of Adult Continuing Education, inspired us with their work on motivation and the media. Andrew Maginn and his team, from the Institute for Employment Studies, drew on their wide experience and earlier work with the learning difficulties and/or disabilities committee to create *Identifying and Addressing Needs – A practical guide*.

Jane Cowell's skills and knowledge proved invaluable, in particular, in the work to develop strategic partnerships. She also brought warmth, humanity and good humour to all our discussions.

We have received immense support from the staff of the Council. Much of the report is underpinned by research undertaken by a group of fabulous women from within the Council. The team from the Council's inspectorate: Vivien Bailey, Toni Fazaeli, Carole Millington, Sara Mogel and Clare Snowdon, which was led initially by Janice Shiner, and then by Merillie Vaughan Huxley, undertook specialist research and analysed inspectorate evidence. The analysis of the individualised student record and other data by Caroline Kempner and Sian Downing of the research and statistics team, unearthed some rich seams of evidence. Avril Ward and her team from the Council's library provided support and expertise throughout.

The work was held together over the two years by Sandra Crowder and Emily Thrane. Sandra was forever patient and painstaking, working magical convergence with diaries and schedules. I am deeply indebted to Emily for insight and clarity. She sustained and informed my understanding of further education and was unflagging in her support.

Helena Kennedy QC
Chairman

June 1997

Introduction

'Further education is everything that does not happen in schools or universities'

This was the throwaway definition I was given when, as a member of the widening participation committee, I sought to circumscribe the parameters of our enquiry. Given the productive relationships which exist between colleges and schools, and the growing opportunities for colleges and higher education institutions to work together, it became clear that even this rough and ready guidance missed the mark. Defining further education exhaustively would be God's own challenge because it is such a large and fertile section of the education world. Yet, despite the formidable role played by further education, it is the least understood and celebrated part of the learning tapestry.

Further education suffers because of prevailing British attitudes. Not only does there remain a very carefully calibrated hierarchy of worthwhile achievement, which has clearly established routes and which privileges academic success well above any other accomplishment, but there is also an appalling ignorance amongst decision-makers and opinion-formers about what goes on in further education. It is so alien to their experience.

Further education's reach is extensive. It has been at the heart of vocational training in a multiplicity of forms – full-time study, part-time study, evening class and day release, in the workplace and out of it. It is the first choice for many young people at 16. Adult education classes have meant added enrichment for many who have already benefited from education and see continuous learning as one of life's pleasures. Further education has been an alternative route to success for many young people who have foundered in the school system, frequently providing another avenue to university education.

It is further education which has invariably given second chances to those who were forced by necessity to make unfulfilling choices. It said 'try again' to those who were labelled as failures and who had decided education was not for the likes of them. It is here, above all, that opportunities have been provided for those caught in the cycle of low-skilled jobs and unemployment who want to better themselves; here, that so many can train or retrain; here, that there is work with refugees and members of immigrant groups to acquire English language skills, or with ex-offenders to facilitate rehabilitation, or with underachievers to fulfil their potential. It is because the achievements in further education are so rarely lauded that we have failed to recognise further education's potential as a vital engine not only of economic renewal but of social cohesion.

Like most parts of the education firmament, the further education sector has gone through a period of dramatic change. The late eighties saw a political drive to end what was perceived as 'producer' dominance in education, substituting for it the principles of the market and competition. There was also a clear decision to reduce the status and powers of local authorities; further education was taken out of local education authority control and the Further Education Funding Council was created. Over a five-year period, there was a profound shift in the control of education from local to central government. These developments went hand-in-hand with a growing recognition by employers and trade unions that a quantum leap was needed in Britain's performance in education and training. Britain was sliding inexorably down the international league tables auguring a low-skill, low-pay economy by the year 2000, unless a skills revolution took place. In an increasingly competitive world, people were recognised as the only source of sustainable competitive advantage; the potential of all our people had to be tapped.

In keeping with the spirit of the times, the Further Education Funding Council placed growth at the heart of its funding methodology and the whole machinery was designed to stimulate expansion.

Growth has indeed taken place at an impressive pace and it is to the credit of colleges and other providers that they rose to the challenge which was set. Many colleges have relished their autonomy, and have proved they can be entrepreneurial in the running of colleges and inventive in their pursuit of new students. There has been a significant increase in efficiency.

However, there is also growing disquiet that the new ethos has encouraged colleges not just to be businesslike but to perform as if they were businesses.

Since funding has been related to to successful outcomes, namely qualifications attained by students, there has been a tendency for too many colleges to go in pursuit of the students who are most likely to succeed. There has been growth, but the students recruited have not come from a sufficiently wide cross-section of the community and there is concern that initiatives to include more working-class people, more disaffected young people, more women, more people from ethnic minority groups are being discontinued because they fall through the gaps in the system. Attracting and keeping those for whom learning is a daunting experience is hard work and financially unrewarding. The effort and resources required to support such students on courses receives insufficient recognition in the current funding system.

Competition has been interpreted by some colleges as a spur to go it alone. Other colleges are seen as rivals for students rather than as potential collaborators with whom good practice and a strategic overview can be shared and developed.

This kind of competition in education has often operated to the detriment of the sector and potential learners. As George Soros, the international financier, put it in a recent essay in Atlantic Monthly, when expressing his fears for the capitalist world, 'Too much competition and too little co-operation can cause intolerable inequities and instabilities.'

In fact, many sophisticated business enterprises now work with their competitors in establishing market share and quality products, as car manufacturers did in the creation and promotion of their 'people carriers'.

However, in the rush away from planning and the heavy hand of the state, no clear strategic overview was developed, nor any statement of an overarching common purpose made. The way of avoiding destructive competition in the public sector is to bring people together around a clear and urgent common purpose. A process of continuous discussion creates alignments and collaborations as the sensible answer to the challenge.

The franchising of provision has shown its potential to reach out to many who have previously been excluded or missed out or who want to advance their skills. Indeed, franchising to community organisations has already had some real success. However, franchising has also been troubled by a failure to recognise that following demand, in true business style, is not the only criterion when funding comes from the public purse. Responsibility to that fund has to underlie public service decisions. Questions have to be asked about the relative priority accorded to public subsidy of employers' job-related training at a time when money is so desperately needed in pursuit of other learning gains. There are other ways of supporting and fostering employers' contributions to learning.

For the overwhelming majority of colleges, the driving force for excellence remains the provision of a non-discriminatory service to all sections of the community. The hallmark of a college's success is, as it should be, public trust, satisfaction of the 'stakeholders' and esteem rather than profitability. These colleges do not see their students as 'consumers', or learning merely as 'training'. They see education as being more than the acquisition of knowledge and skills. In a system so caught up in what is measurable, we can forget that learning is also about problem-solving, learning to learn, acquiring the capability for intelligent choice in exercising personal responsibility. It is a weapon against poverty. It is the route to participation and active citizenship.

These values are not a substitute for good management, efficiency and fine teaching, all of which should be imperative in an effective institution. However, public service values, which have been the pulse of further education, are finding little articulation in the new language of the market.

A well-run, private-sector business continuously finds new means of being more profitable. It will aim to sell what brings in most money. It is bad business practice to subsidise that which is unprofitable. However, many colleges want to include activities which, although unprofitable in the strict sense, are of value to the community. They know they can play a part in drawing back to the social embrace many who are disaffected. They want genuine open access to education and training for all sections of the community. They want to underpin employers' long-term competitive capability by assisting in the skilling of the workforce.

The 'market' may not be predisposed to support and pay for such educational activities, but they demonstrate the public service ethos of the colleges. It is this ethos which helps to earn public trust, esteem and, potentially, public support.

All the public services – the National Health Service, social and education services – are struggling in this time of change to forge a new synthesis, a blend which is true to the public service ethos with its commitment to 'the public good', but at the same time exploits business as a fruitful model of effectiveness. Finding that synergy in the right balance is one of the 'wicked' problems facing educators; to achieve it the purpose of education and the values which underpin it have to be made clear.

Education must be at the heart of any inspired project for regeneration in Britain. It should be a springboard for the revitalisation that our communities so urgently need. However, in all the political debates, it is the economic rationale for increasing participation in education which has been paramount. Prosperity depends upon there being a vibrant economy, but an economy which regards its own success as the highest good is a dangerous one. Justice and equity must also have their claim upon the arguments for educational growth. In a social landscape where there is a growing gulf between those who have and those who have not, the importance of social cohesion cannot be ignored.

Making social cohesion a prominent goal of education also has a powerful rationale in economic terms. There has been a growing acceptance by economists of the centrality of human and social capital in economic success. Today, capital is embodied increasingly in the knowledge and skills of human beings rather than in factories, machinery and plant. There is also growing recognition internationally that economic success is inextricably bound up with social factors. The American sociologists, James Coleman and Robert Putnam, and the political analyst Francis Fuykayama all argue that law, contract and economic rationality provide a necessary but insufficient basis for the stability and prosperity of post-industrial societies; these must also be leavened with reciprocity, moral obligation, duty towards community and trust. It is this 'social capital' which has a large and measurable economic value. A nation's well-being, as well as its ability to compete, is conditioned by a single pervasive cultural characteristic – the level of social capital inherent in the society.

When people trust government to act in their interests and for the common good, they themselves are happy to give something in return. When people join together in common endeavour, they create the subsoil in which growth and development can take place.

Education has always been a source of social vitality and the more people we can include in the community of learning, the greater the benefits to us all. The very process involves interaction between people; it is the means by which the values and wisdom of a society are shared and transmitted across the generations. Education strengthens the ties which bind people, takes the fear out of difference and encourages tolerance. It helps people to see what makes the world tick and the ways in which they, individually and together, can make a difference. It is the likeliest means of creating a modern, well-skilled workforce, reducing levels of crime, and creating participating citizens.

The parents I saw on a Knowsley housing estate, which has very high unemployment, came to basic skills classes in the family room of the local primary school. They grew in confidence, felt more comfortable in school precincts and became active in the parent-teacher association. Their interest in the education of their children and their ability to help their children learn increased dramatically.

The employees involved in the educational development schemes at Ford or Unipart may not be learning anything directly connected to their job. However, simply by engaging in the learning process their self-worth and capabilities are improved and, as a result, their contribution to, and overall effectiveness for, the organisation are enormous. Their own employability is also greatly enhanced.

Government has the key role in presenting the powerful vision of a 'learning nation'. For Britain, this means the creation of a new philosophy about the purposes of education. It means we must all see ourselves as in the picture, capable always of new learning. Perhaps the goal should be that each and every one of us should learn something new by the year 2000. 'Learning Gain' should be on a par with getting fit and just as ready a subject of conversation.

Corporations should be propelled into a competitive drive to bring learning into the workplace, with trade unions and employers collaborating in the endeavour.

Lifelong learning does not just happen in colleges. Indeed, with the revolutionary advances of technology, bricks and mortar are increasingly becoming less significant in the whole business of learning.

There are many providers and locations, including the home and the workplace, training and enterprise councils, and schools and community centres, where people expand their horizons and extend their capabilities.

For many men, the experience of job redundancy and unemployment is so totally undermining of their sense of masculinity that the means of luring them back into education have to be sensitive to their shattered confidence. The trick is to bring learning to learners wherever they are, whether it be in family rooms in primary schools, libraries, betting shops, snooker halls, rooms above pubs, or shopping malls. Adult learners often prefer to study alongside their peers. Women returners blossom in courses specifically designed for them. Success also comes from making the learning feel real and relevant to people's lives.

Our inventiveness should see no limits in creating all kinds of community learning centres which feel right to the user. It should be one of our aims that half of the largest corporations and public sector employers are equipped with learning resource centres within the next twenty years; 50,000 centres would cover a third of the workforce. These centres should be part of the new 'University for Industry'.

The 'Pathways for Learning', which are recommended, are not yet more qualifications to be showered upon a system already overburdened with them in all shapes and sizes. The 'Pathways' represent a commitment and a quality promise to any learner that a suitable, supported route back into learning will be available. For some, it will be at a basic level; for others, it will mean coming in at a higher level. Many of the latter will have been out of the system for a long time, or will be wary of it and need a different compass to negotiate the terrain.

The ways will be many and varied and colleges will be expected to conjure up their own initiatives in response to the identified needs in their area. One of our key proposals is the establishment of a national network of strategic partnerships to work together in promoting learning amongst a wider public.

Opportunities have to be seized to stimulate a broad and large demand which can be either delivered by further education, or supported by it, or enabled by a collaboration of providers. There is absolutely nowhere that can claim it is already meeting the challenge completely. Unless participants get what they want, where they want it, at the right cost, we will not get the widening of participation to the degree needed.

Lifelong inclusive learning becomes meaningless rhetoric if money is not available to make such a grand project a reality. And it is a grand project if it is to be real.

There is public consensus that education needs more money and that the quantum has to be increased. But, in the clamour for funds, further education's claims have been sidelined. The education of the nation's children is obviously a foremost consideration. However, serious inequity exists in the financing of post-16 education.

Only a quarter of the five million post-16 learners in England attend universities. Yet two thirds of the post-school education budget is spent on the universities.

Even with the exciting expansion of further and higher education, the children of the working class have not been the real beneficiaries. Children from my own class background are still not participating. Sixty-two per cent of university students come from social classes I and II. One per cent come from social class V.

Investment in further education is one of the most cost-effective ways of tackling the cumulative effects of learning failure. It is undoubtedly the best way to remedy past deficiencies.

Yet the shocking fact is that support for students is heavily weighted towards those who personally go on to benefit most from their education and whose family circumstances are most favourable to continuing in education. One fifth of the households which have the highest incomes in our country receive more in educational subsidies than those forming either of the bottom two fifths.

Like the trickle-down theory of economics, there is a trickle-down theory of education which relies upon the notion that concentrating the bulk of educational investment on our top cohorts produces an excellence which permeates the system. For centuries, this thinking has blighted not just the British economy, but the whole of British life. It demands an urgent reappraisal.

There has to be a redistribution of resources in favour of further education if learning is really to be the engine of economic and social success. This will involve government taking some tough decisions affecting the gold card of funding for full-time higher education. We have to move towards equity of funding for post-16 education.

The higher education sector is facing its own financial hardship, as I know from my role as chancellor of one of the new universities. An injection of money is needed for higher education to maintain high quality and international esteem and this is being addressed by the Dearing review. Our universities are the best in the world and that pre-eminence must be preserved. What is needed is the same excellence to be pursued on behalf of students in other parts of the firmament. The Treasury has to find more money for education and further education has to move up the agenda in making a claim on those funds.

If government is committed to widening participation, it has to be prepared for some financial redistribution. It has to increase the quantum for further education and increase access funds. The ladders linking further education and higher education are extending all the time, and higher education will increasingly be delivered by the further education sector. This will be an economical way of expanding and encouraging participation in ongoing cumulative learning. But there is a bigger picture.

Most adults receive no further learning opportunities after completing their initial education and training. Over half our young people come out of school and start adult life in need of compensatory education. Clearly, this cries out for the proper resourcing of schools and the improvement of standards; but if we want to thrive economically, it also cries out for an attack upon the backlog of thwarted potential which can properly be met only by further education.

None of us is oblivious to the problems in finding money, and it is for this reason that we recommend to government a number of innovative strategies. One is the establishment of a 'Learning Regeneration Fund' to operate at regional and subregional levels. The fund would draw together pockets of money from the Department of Trade and Industry, the Department of Education and Employment, the Single Regeneration Budget, the Funding Councils for Further and Higher Education, European regeneration money and private sector contributions. It would be drawn upon by the local partnerships to pump-prime projects directed at widening participation in learning.

The second initiative involves lottery funds. If ever there was a use to which lottery money should be put this is it – the creation of a fund for widening participation in education, by harnessing new technology and drawing in those who have never participated before. One fifth of the lottery profits are currently taken up by 'Millennium' projects. As we enter the new century, this allocation will become available for other uses. We propose that the money is captured for the launch of a government campaign called 'Learning into the New Millennium' with the creation of a 'Learning Nation Fund'.

Lottery funds have to be spent on projects additional to those which should be paid for out of ordinary departmental budgets. No issues of additionality arise with this proposal because the money will be used to bring into post-compulsory education those who do not currently take part. The very people who spend most money on the lottery would be those who benefited. The justice of the case is overwhelming.

It was also clear to the committee that the Further Education Funding Council has to create financial incentives to enable colleges to expand their missions. The current funding methodology of the Council is under review. After consulting the sector, the Council may endorse the present formula or recommend change. Either way, the further education world has to set its priorities with widening participation at its heart. In a system based upon units, the student who is at present excluded has to be 'unit-rich' if providers are to respond. Levers which exist within the current funding methodology can readily be used to move this work from the margins to the mainstream of funding.

The benefits system also cries out for reform. It is ridiculous that a system of social security should inhibit rather than facilitate learning as a progression to work. A government that is committed to initiating a 'welfare to work' programme should also introduce a 'welfare to learning' programme.

My recent journeys in the world of further education have provided me with a thousand and one histories of changed lives. As with most good stories, they usually describe the conquering of fear, a battle against odds, the discovery of self, as well as the acquisition of skills and knowledge. I like to imagine that like 'Scheherazade' I could captivate you with these accounts, all of which testify to the transformative power of learning. Some are about the precious acquisition of basic literacy, others about studying to degree level using the ladders provided by further education. The variables are countless but the excitement of success is infectious. For those involved in education these accounts are happily familiar.

These stories are what education is all about. They feed the commitment and idealism which is still so strong amongst educators and they fuel the desire for radical change which the committee came to share.

The Agenda for Change

- Launch government campaign 'Learning into the New Millennium: the Creation of a Learning Nation'

- Dedicate lottery funding to launch the 'Learning into the New Millennium' initiative

- Prioritise widening participation in the post-16 education agenda

- Redistribute public resources towards those with less success in earlier learning, moving towards equity of funding in post-16 education

- Establish a lifetime entitlement to education up to level 3, which is free for young people and those who are socially and economically deprived

- Create a national network of strategic partnerships to identify local need, stimulate demand, respond creatively and promote learning

- Encourage employers to provide learning centres linked to the 'University for Industry'; large firms would have to have their own, small firms would need to work together or with larger firms

- Reform the Council's funding mechanism to recognise levels of previous achievement and social and economic deprivation

- Create an expanded Council 'Access and Childcare Fund'

- Harness new technology for learning

- Launch a credit accumulation system, to be operative within five years

- Create new 'Pathways to Learning' – a unitised system for recognising achievement

- Take learning to the learner
- Reform financial support to students, including the benefit system in the interests of equity and promoting 'Welfare to Work through Learning'
- Launch a 'Charter for Learning'
- Create a 'Learning Regeneration Fund' at regional and subregional levels
- Establish a legal duty upon television to educate
- Set new national learning targets and local targets for participation.

I The case for widening participation is irresistible

Learning is central to economic prosperity and social cohesion

Equity dictates that all should have the opportunity to succeed

A dramatic shift in policy is required to widen participation in post-16 learning and to create a self-perpetuating learning society

Summary

Learning is central to economic success and social cohesion. As we approach the twenty-first century and the immense challenges of the global economy and unprecedented technological change, achieving these inseparable national goals will depend more and more on the knowledge, understanding and skills of the whole population. Recent policies to increase participation and achievement in learning have achieved some success, but mainly in providing opportunities for those who have already achieved to continue to do so. Those who are disadvantaged educationally are also disadvantaged economically and socially; equity and viability dictate that all should have the opportunity to succeed. To continue with current policy at a time of rapid change will widen the gulf between those who succeed in learning and those who do not, and puts at risk both social unity and economic prosperity. We are convinced that national leadership is required to place learning at the heart of our national common purpose. We must widen participation not simply increase it. Widening participation means increasing access to learning and providing opportunities for success and progression to a much wider cross-section of the population than now. All those who are not fulfilling their potential or who have underachieved in the past must be drawn into successful learning. Widening participation in post-16 learning will create a self-perpetuating learning society.

Recommendations

The government should:

- provide leadership to place the creation of a self-perpetuating learning society at the heart of the national common purpose

- create a national strategy for post-16 learning to widen not simply increase participation

- state its aspiration for all to achieve a level 3 qualification including key skills to provide the platform for the creation of a self-perpetuating learning society

- set new and comprehensive 'National Learning Targets'

- expect local partnerships to set local participation targets

- accelerate its activities to harmonise systems for measuring participation and achievement in post-16 learning and publish an annual report on progress in participation and achievement.

The Council should:

- publish an annual report on progress in widening participation in the further education sector using the new framework for measurement that has been developed by the committee.

Learning for Work and Learning for Life are Inseparable

Our work over the last two years has confirmed our conviction that learning is central both to economic prosperity and the health of society. We believe that the achievement of economic goals and social cohesion are intertwined. A healthy society is a necessary condition for a thriving economy: where parents encourage and support their children's education; where people in employment can adapt to change; where enterprise can flourish and where those seeking employment can acquire the skills they need for economic activity. Equally, economic prosperity is a major factor in enabling individuals, families and communities to play a full part in the personal, social and cultural dimensions of life.

Many of the skills and qualities required for success at work are the same as those required for success in personal, social and community terms. Literacy, numeracy, communication and information technology, together with problem-solving skills and effective team-working, are widely recognised as key skills for employment. These capabilities are learned and developed in a wide variety of ways over a lifetime. Participation in community life, be it working in a charity shop, serving as a school governor, managing a local football team or joining a mother-and-toddler group provide rich, diverse and accessible routes for learning. Those without these key capabilities will find themselves at a disadvantage in social and public life as well as in the labour market.

All Learning is Valuable

We believe that all types of learning are valuable. It has always been difficult to define 'vocational' and 'non-vocational' learning and these concepts are fast becoming less and less valid. The growth of leisure, tourism and entertainment industries means that more and more people are making their living from other people's leisure pursuits. Many of them may have discovered a new career direction through their own leisure interests. Equally, many people pursue formal qualifications for personal satisfaction whereas the student in the conversational Spanish class may really have an eye on applying for a job in the export section of their organisation. The student taking an upholstery course to re-cover the family's old sofa may later set up a business using such newly-acquired skills. The distinction between training by employers, and education by educational institutions has also become blurred by the growth of work-based learning and employee development schemes.

The Challenge of Change

Even a glimpse of the future provides incontrovertible evidence that we must widen our horizons. The pace of technological innovation within the world of work continues to accelerate phenomenally quickly. Changes in information technology are akin to the introduction of the printing press and the industrial revolution, both of which precipitated revolutions in the spread of learning. More and more people need to achieve higher-level knowledge, understanding and skills. Everyone must acquire different knowledge, improved understanding and new skills throughout their working lives. Failure to take this agenda will worsen the already wide gap between those people and their families who know and can do, and those who do not know and cannot do.

Conventional structures of work are changing at a rapid rate. More people are working in small organisations, on part-time or fixed-term contracts, or on a self-employed basis. Long-term trends identified by the Confederation of British Industry and the Institute of Employment Studies indicate that an increasing proportion of the workforce, currently almost one in four, will become part-time or temporary workers. New and more flexible styles of working will bring with them different or additional demands for learning opportunities for self-management, work and business planning as these groups of workers become increasingly common. More people will work from home and will need to learn how to manage their own activities or to plan their own businesses.

Developments in new technology impact on domestic and community life as well as on the workplace. Next year, more personal computers will be sold in the world than television sets. Multi-media computers will soon be available for the same price as video recorders and many more people will be able to afford them. Routine activities such as shopping, booking appointments for health care and other services may soon commonly be carried out using home-based computers. Social changes also precipitate new learning needs; for example, the growth of private pensions and the introduction of self-assessment of income tax will bring with them a need for increased knowledge and skills. Technology, both in the home and the workplace, provides new and powerful ways to develop more widely the demand and the opportunity for learning.

Meeting the Challenge

The 'National Targets for Education and Training' were launched by the Confederation of British Industry in 1991. In 1995, the National Advisory Council for Education and Training Targets (NACETT) published revised national foundation and lifetime targets for the year 2000 under the banner, 'Developing skills for a successful future'. Despite recent increases in participation, achieving the national targets is still an enormous challenge. NACETT reported in July 1996 that an additional 100,000 young people under 19 would need to achieve foundation target 1 if the 85 per cent target was to be met by the year 2000.[1] Lifetime target 1 is that three out of five of the adult workforce should be qualified to at least the equivalent of NVQ level 3. Only two in five of the workforce were qualified to this level in autumn 1995. To meet the targets for the year 2000, we need over a million adults to achieve level 3 qualifications each year between now and the end of the century.[2]

Achieving the current targets remains a significant challenge. The urgency of the task is plain. The United Kingdom's partners and competitors are not standing still. If we wish even to maintain our competitive position, we will soon have to achieve levels of training which are way beyond the present national and local targets.

Measuring Participation and Achievement

Measuring participation and achievement in post-16 education and training is not straightforward. Schools, colleges and private training providers have different systems for collecting data. There is little detailed information on the training carried out by employers. It is not possible to get a comprehensive picture of levels of participation and achievement, or of changes in these over time. The government's plans to improve the collection of national data should be accelerated. Comprehensive reports on participation and achievement should be published annually.

Participation in post-16 learning has increased significantly in recent years.

However, there is clear evidence that policies which are directed solely at increasing participation will not achieve the levels of learning and achievement now required, and certainly not those to which we aspire:

- in 1995 under half of 15 year olds achieved five GCSEs at grade C or above [3]

- although more than four in five 16 year olds stayed on in full-time or part-time education, or were involved in work-based training, this applied to only three out of five 18 year olds [4]

- just over two out of five young people left 'Youth Training' with a qualification in 1995-96 [5]

- over four out of five students in the college sector completed courses in 1994-95; two in three of those who completed their courses achieved a qualification

- less than 44 per cent of employees receive training. [6]

Groups Not Participating and Not Achieving

There is no single source of evidence to identify those who do not participate in learning and those who fail to achieve. However, an accumulation of evidence points in the same direction.

There are two ways of identifying the groups which do not participate. One way is to look at specific characteristics such as age, sex, or ethnicity. We know that employers provide less training to older workers than younger workers, and that women and members of some ethnic minority groups generally have fewer qualifications. Participation by these groups is changing. More women than men now participate in post-16 education and young people from certain ethnic groups are more likely to be in full-time education than their white peers.[7] Furthermore, there are very different patterns of participation in some localities. In some communities, the most significant under-representation may be among white working-class males; in others, it may be older women from ethnic minority groups. The other way of identifying such groups is to look at general characteristics such as levels of previous educational achievement, or levels of income, or where people live. We discovered that this method applies both locally and nationally. It also stands the test of time.

If at first you don't succeed . . . you don't succeed

Studies consistently demonstrate that qualifications earned at 16 provide an excellent predictor of whether a young person will continue in full-time learning and that good academic performance at 16 notably reduces the impact on participation of other factors such as sex, family occupational background, ethnicity and school sector.[8]

Those who enter higher education as full-time students have already achieved academic success. Most will go on to achieve financial success too. On average graduates earn over half as much again as those qualified to level 3, and nearly twice as much as those with no qualifications.[9] Despite the dramatic increase in the number of young and mature people entering higher education, the socio-economic profile of higher education students has not changed significantly.[10]

Those with high levels of qualifications are more likely than those with low or no qualifications to receive job-related training from their employer[11] and are also more likely to take the initiative in seeking learning opportunities.

Those in the college sector who entered college with low levels of achievement tend to have higher drop-out rates and lower levels of achievement when leaving college than other students.[12]

Unemployment is experienced disproportionately by unskilled and semi-skilled people; evidence suggests that people are less likely to seek learning opportunities whilst unemployed than when in work.[13] Those who do study whilst unemployed tend to be young – rates peak among those aged 25-34 – and they are more likely to possess a qualification.[14]

One in six of the population over the age of 16 has serious problems with basic skills.[15]

All the evidence suggests that it is those who are already well qualified who go on to earn more and to demand and get more learning; many of those who fail the first time round never make up the lost ground, educationally or economically. There are clear links between previous educational achievement and economic and social disadvantage. The link between staying on in education, GCSE results and economic and social disadvantage at 16 is well established, though the link does not apply for the work-based route. Council statistics show that, for both adults and young people, there are strong links between economic disadvantage and low income on the one hand, and poor retention rates and low levels of achievement on the other.[16]

We are convinced by the wide-ranging and detailed evidence presented to us that there exists an immense and diverse body of people in this country which should be encouraged and welcomed into post-16 learning.

Participation Must be Widened, Not Simply Increased

Equity dictates that all should have the opportunity to succeed in personal, social and economic spheres. Collective economic success will depend on maximising the potential of all; it will not be enough to draw on the talents of an educated elite or even of an educated majority. As prosperity comes to depend more and more on knowledge and skills, any economy in which 30 per cent of its people fail to maximise their potential or do not develop learning skills, will, in the long run, lose out in competition with those who take a more comprehensive approach. Developing the capacity of everyone to contribute to and benefit from the economic, personal, social and cultural dimensions of their lives is central to achieving the whole range of goals we set ourselves as a nation. In our view, public policy for post-compulsory learning must be dramatically, systematically and consistently redirected towards widening rather than simply increasing participation and achievement. A much wider cross-section of the population needs to be involved than now.

We found that while recent policy acknowledges both the economic and social benefits of learning, it does not recognise sufficiently their interdependence. The result is that priority in further education is given to economic goals at the expense of learning for life. We believe there are two major weaknesses in this approach; there is too limited a definition of learners, and too narrow a focus on the range of learning opportunities. Despite their inclusive aims, the national targets for lifetime education apply only to the workforce, not to those who are unemployed and economically inactive. The acquisition of basic skills, study units which lead to qualifications, and uncertificated learning are the ladders leading to the achievement of these targets. New and more comprehensive 'National Learning Targets' are required which include these important steps and are supported by local participation targets.

A Self-perpetuating Learning Society

The pace of change in the economy, and in society more widely, is such that we will all need to develop and add to our work skills. The ability to learn is the most important skill and the central thrust of public policy for learning should be the development of the capacity to learn throughout life. The key to developing a society of learners is the recognition of a universal entitlement for all to acquire a level 3 qualification, including appropriate key skills. Such an entitlement could provide a platform for lifelong learning and for employment.

National Leadership

Government must apply imaginative national leadership in creating a learning society at the heart of its common purpose for the nation. There must be a national strategy to re-energise the efforts of the key stakeholders in learning.

A national strategy should be underpinned by a framework designed to measure whether participation in learning is being widened. The framework should provide a consistent method of measuring progress, while at the same time allowing enough flexibility to take account of local priorities. We have developed a specific framework for the Council to use in measuring progress in the further education sector.

Endnotes

1   Five GCSEs at grade C or above, intermediate GNVQ or NVQ level 2

2   Skills for 2000: Supplement to the report on progress towards the national targets for education and training, National Advisory Council for Education and Training Targets, London, 1996

3   Department for Education and Employment, Secondary school performance tables 1995, DfEE, London, 1995

4   Skills for 2000: Supplement to the report on progress towards the national targets for education and training, National Advisory Council for Education and Training Targets, London, 1996

5   UK Parliament (DfEE), Financial Control of Payments made under the Training for Work and Youth Training Programmes in England, The Stationery Office, London, 1997

6   Skills for 2000: Supplement to the report on progress towards the national targets for education and training, National Advisory Council for Education and Training Targets, London, 1996

7   Skills for 2000: Supplement to the report on progress towards the national targets for education and training, National Advisory Council for Education and Training Targets, London, 1996

8   Employment Department Youth Cohort Study, cited in Hilary Steedman and Andy Green, *Widening Participation in Further Education and Training: A Survey of the Issues*, Centre for Economic Performance, London, 1996

9   General Household Survey, quoted in *Basic Skills for Life*, DfEE, London, 1997

10 Tony Uden, Widening Participation: Routes to a Learning Society: A policy discussion paper, NIACE, Leicester, 1996

11 Training Statistics 1996, DfEE Statistical Volume, The Stationery Office, London, 1996

12 Council statistical evidence commissioned by the committee

13 Veronica McGivney, Motivating Unemployed Adults to Undertake Education and Training: Some British and Other European Findings, NIACE, Leicester, 1992

14 David Bottomley, Stephen McKay and Robert Walker, Unemployment and Jobseeking: a national survey 1995, Research Report No. 62, Department of Social Security and The Stationery Office, London, 1997

15 Basic Skills Agency evidence to the committee

16 Council statistical evidence commissioned by the committee

2 The national strategy for widening participation must have further education at its core

The unique contribution of further education at the heart of a self-perpetuating learning society must be recognised and celebrated

Only further education can deliver to all the entitlement to have an opportunity to achieve level 3

A consistent national policy framework must be created to develop the richness and diversity of further education

Summary

We are convinced that further education has a unique contribution to make to widening participation in post-16 learning and the creation of a self-perpetuating learning society. It has a key role to play in reaching out to all those who need to be engaged if the aspiration for all to achieve level 3 is to be achieved. It offers first-choice and second-chance learning opportunities for young people. Its diversity means it has the potential to reach out to adults who can become new learners in their homes, in factories, in shops and offices, in the schools where their children learn and in a host of community venues. It can offer a variety of first steps or starting points for learners. It can offer updating for those in and out of work, and an impressive and comprehensive range of progression routes, reaching to higher education and beyond. Further education, however, requires a consistent policy framework if its full potential is to be realised.

Recommendations

The government should:

- recognise and celebrate the unique contribution that further education can make to widening participation

- create a consistent policy framework for publicly-funded further education which embraces planning, funding, quality assessment, measurement of performance, financial support for students, guidance and the means of stimulating demand for learning

- promote the establishment of employers' learning centres as part of the 'University for Industry'; firms with over 200 employees should set up their new centres, and smaller firms should be encouraged to work together to create them

- encourage local partnerships to identify openings for introducing new employee development schemes

- encourage local education authorities to produce annual development plans setting out their proposals for securing adequate provision for non-schedule 2 students

- explore urgently all avenues for ensuring the availability of adequate funding for non-schedule 2 provision, including alternative funding routes.

The Council should:

- include in the criteria for schedule 2(d) provision, any non-schedule 2 provision which is specifically planned to act as a first step towards embarking on schedule 2 provision.

All Have Parts to Play

All those involved in education and training in the country have parts to play in widening participation. Schools have a crucial role in providing the foundations for a learning society by increasing the numbers of young people achieving at level 2.

The United Kingdom maintains a strong position in higher education and these institutions too must open their doors to a much wider cross-section of the population. We look forward to the findings of the National Committee of Inquiry into Higher Education which will report in July 1997 on how higher education might be developed over the next twenty years.

Further Education is at the Heart of a Self-perpetuating Learning Society

Further education is often viewed as education which takes place in colleges of further education. From the outset, we were convinced that we needed to define further education more broadly if we were to look seriously at widening participation. Positioned between schools and higher education, and overlapping both, is a rich, diverse and exciting range of provision, providers and delivery modes. Significant further education provision exists in both schools and higher education institutions and substantial higher education provision is delivered by further education providers. We were convinced that widening participation required us to include in our work the full range of further education provision and providers. Hence we arrived at the following working definitions:

Definitions

- **post-16 learning** refers to all providers and provision outside compulsory schooling

- **further education** refers to all further education provision whether in school sixth forms, further education and sixth form colleges, local education authority adult and community education services, voluntary and community organisations. It also includes some provision which is offered in the higher education sector, by employers and trade unions, or by independent training providers

- **the further education sector** refers to further education colleges and any other institutions funded by the Council

- **the college sector** refers to further education colleges.

Further education is the key to widening participation. Its contributions are the general, academic and transferable vocational learning leading to the level 3 platform needed to widen participation. The further education sector provides progression opportunities that a self-perpetuating learning society will increasingly need, including vocational and academic higher education. It is fertile ground for imaginative public and private partnerships based on shared commitment to raising aspirations and the value of learning. These partnerships have the potential to break through existing barriers and deliver the widening of participation. Our conviction is that the urgent and immediate priority is to enable all to have the opportunity to achieve level 3 and that this aim can only be achieved by further education. Not only will further education provide a means of bringing all to the level 3 platform, it will provide the most cost-effective way of broadening the entry base for higher education.

Further Education for Young People

We have highlighted our great concern that over half our young people leave school without the initial foundation platform of five GCSEs at grade C or above. The aspiration to increase achievement in schools should be that all young people are qualified and eager to succeed at level 3. Achieving the aspiration will take time. The impact of low achievement on young people's prospects for continued participation and achievement in learning throughout their lives is clear. Further education has the capacity to engage and re-engage them, through a wide choice of basic skills, academic, vocational and pre-vocational routes in formal, informal and workplace settings.

In our interim report, *Pathways to Success*, we welcomed the white paper *Learning to Compete*, which responded to some of the committee's concerns in relation to participation by young people. The establishment of an entitlement to career planning and learning opportunities up to level 3, and the introduction of formalised partnership approaches through the 'Relaunch Strategy', closely reflected our own conclusions on the way forward in responding to the needs of some of these young people. We also welcome the policies of the new government which promise to bring new hope and learning opportunities to school-leavers in the future, and to those who left school recently and who are now out of work.

Further Education for Adults

We need to tackle urgently the enormous backlog caused by decades of under-achievement in which national strategies for education and training have failed to make significant inroads. The immediate needs of the three out of five adults without qualifications at level 3 cannot be addressed either by schools or by higher education institutions. Widening participation for adults is by no means restricted to second-chance education. Adults, including those who have already gained degrees, need to continue learning if they are to benefit fully economically, socially and culturally.

Learning may be undertaken: to maintain or enhance employment prospects; to support children in their reading; to care for an elderly relative; to plan for retirement; to budget on a reduced income. Learning may also be undertaken for fun, for personal development or to achieve an appreciation of broader issues. Adults may be motivated to learn for many different reasons at different times in their lives. Further education with its comprehensive curriculum, and its diversity and richness is uniquely placed to respond to this challenge.

Richness and Diversity

The further education curriculum is immense and wide-ranging. Some people need to acquire basic skills as a first step to learning. Others need support with basic skills as they follow their learning programme. Basic skills courses are widely available in colleges, adult centres and community locations. Increasingly, providers are working in partnership with employers to deliver basic skills within the workplace. Video-conferencing is used to deliver basic skills in community settings.

The Linwood Centre

The adult basic education service run by Charles Keene College operates a family literacy project at The Linwood Centre. The project is based on a housing estate on the outskirts of Leicester which has high levels of unemployment. Family literacy courses are designed to develop parents' skills by helping them become more involved in their children's education. Parents make work and picture books, write stories and read them to their children. They have developed their skills by editing and simplifying school documents. This has proved a powerful way to help parents learn about the education system. Several parents have progressed and work as student support staff in schools. Some serve as school governors. One is the chair of governors at a local school.

Further education offers a broad range of general programmes which do not lead to qualifications. These programmes provide locally-accessible learning opportunities for personal development, and the achievement of social and community goals. These enable people to develop specific knowledge, skills and understanding together with the key skills involved in learning. For some adult learners, such programmes provide an important first step in returning to learning.

Hackney Community College

Hackney Community College has developed a mapping system to develop clear progression routes from community-based 'leisure' courses to accredited programmes. A handbook provides information about each type of course and sets out related subjects and progression opportunities in and outside the college. The maps have been put on a database with graphics, music and a touch-sensitive screen. Part-time adult education tutors have been trained in the use of the maps. College records show that 14 per cent of students in non-schedule 2 courses in 1995-96 progressed to schedule 2 courses, often in unrelated subjects.

The further education portfolio includes a variety of programmes designed to engage and support adults returning to education. These 'access' programmes enable learners to develop skills and confidence in learning, to sample different occupational and subject areas and to construct plans for continued learning. Increasingly, such programmes offer accreditation to aid progression.

Young people and adults who want an academic route find there is a wide choice of GCE A and A/S levels and GCSEs in further education, along with access to higher education programmes. Many of the academic options are available both full time and part time. They are offered in both daytime and evening sessions, located in a variety of central and community-based venues. For some, these studies will be their first choice; for others, a second chance. When so many have not achieved their potential at school, opportunities for a second chance to pursue an academic education are essential for reasons of equity and economic need.

GNVQs offer preparation for higher education and employment in broad vocational areas. Key skills are integral to GNVQ programmes and are assessed. Whilst work experience is not mandatory, many GNVQ students benefit from periods of work placement. GNVQs offer routes into vocational training and higher education. They provide a real alternative for those who find academic study at level 3 inappropriate to their needs. While most GNVQ programmes are full time, providers have begun to explore the potential for delivering this broad, vocationally-focused programme on a part-time basis.

Further education provides a comprehensive range of vocational training at all levels for both young people and adults. Such training is becoming increasingly flexible in terms of timing, location and delivery. No longer is it restricted to full-time, day or block release and evening provision. More and more it is happening in the workplace, and at weekends, accommodating shift work patterns and capitalising on the enormous opportunities presented by new technology.

The Role of Employers

We are convinced that the continued development of learning in the workplace is central to widening participation. The Investors in People standard is proving a powerful vehicle for demonstrating to employers the links between investment in learning and business success.

Employers play a key role in providing learning opportunities. Expenditure by employers on education and training is broadly estimated at £10.6 billion a year.[1] Employers have been key contributors to the success of 'Modern Apprenticeships'. Imaginative partnerships between employers and providers of training have created new opportunities for learning. Much of the work takes place on employers' premises and students benefit from the expertise of college staff and the use of industry standard facilities. The smallest employers provide the least training; part-time employees and those with low previous attainment are least likely to get training. Many of those currently under-represented in education and training are in work. The workplace is an attractive venue for many to engage in learning and its potential must be further exploited.

Increasingly, employers and trade unions are encouraging employees to take part in learning as part of wider development schemes for employees which are designed to promote the value of learning, to build confidence in the individual's ability to learn and to increase the motivation to learn. Learning centres are being established.

The government should encourage large firms to create their own learning centres. Smaller firms could work together to establish such centres. These centres should be part of the new 'University for Industry' proposed by the government. Local partnerships should be encouraged to identify openings for new employee development schemes.

Chaos and Confusion

Along with the rich choices within further education, there is also a fair amount of chaos and confusion. The drive for diversity has created barriers to access, success and progression. The divisions that exist are sometimes made worse by the way they are managed. These difficulties must be significantly reduced. Collaborative inter-agency approaches should be adopted locally. Government should introduce a consistent national policy framework which recognises the richness and diversity of further education. The framework should embrace planning, funding, quality assessment, performance measurement, financial support for learners, and guidance. It should also stimulate demand for learning.

The Further and Higher Education Act 1992: Schedule 2 and Non-schedule 2 Provision

The *Further and Higher Education Act 1992* formalised the distinction within the further education curriculum between programmes which lead directly or indirectly to qualifications, and those which do not, by dividing responsibility. The Council is charged with securing sufficient and adequate schedule 2 provision; local education authorities are responsible for the adequacy of non-schedule 2 provision.

The creation of this division was controversial at the time and remains so today. Not least, because the planning of accredited training within a nationally-funded system is seen by some as conferring status on such training. We believe that schedule 2 and non-schedule 2 provision must be valued equally. For many 'new' learners, non-schedule 2 courses provide essential first steps to more formal learning and accreditation.

Pressure on local education authority budgets has led, in some parts of the country, to drastic reductions in non-schedule 2 provision. There are those who argue that responsibility should transfer from local government to the Council. This is not our view. We see great advantages in maintaining plurality in further education. The involvement of local education authorities and the exercise of local discretion are valuable in maintaining diversity; further education should continue to be firmly rooted in the local community. However, because non-schedule 2 provision forms such an important element of further education and is so crucial to widening participation in education, we are concerned about the significant reductions by some local education authorities and the increasingly varied extent to which this provision is available. Measures must be taken to reduce this variability. The government should encourage local education authorities to prepare annual development plans setting out their proposals for securing adequate non-schedule 2 provision. All avenues for ensuring that adequate funding is available, including alternative funding routes, should be explored urgently. This could include the routing of funding through the Council. The Council should include in its criteria for schedule 2(d), any non-schedule 2 provision which is specifically planned to act as a first step towards schedule 2 provision.

Endnotes

1   Department for Education and Employment press release, UK Training by Employers, 13 September 1996

3   Market principles alone will not widen participation

Competition in publicly-funded further education has resulted in improved responsiveness

Competition has also inhibited the collaboration needed to widen participation

Partnerships must be created to fill the strategic vacuum at local level

Summary

The introduction of competition in publicly-funded further education has been accompanied by improved responsiveness to learners' needs. Some providers, however, have competed for those students most likely to succeed. Further education needs to expand the demand for learning as a whole. The current model of independent providers steered mainly by a variety of national arrangements does not enable strategic goals to be identified and achieved at local level. Collaborative strategic and operational approaches are needed to identify and address unmet and unexpressed needs and to secure the best value for money from public funds. Community involvement in planning in the further education sector should be increased.

Recommendations

The government should:

- enable the establishment of a national system of permanent local strategic partnerships to widen participation; the partnerships should support the Council in its duty to secure the provision of sufficient and adequate further education

- revise the articles of government of sector colleges to give corporations a responsibility to meet the needs of the local community.

The Council should:

- revise its guidance on strategic planning to reflect the contents of *Identifying and Addressing Needs*, the guide prepared by the Institute of Employment Studies, which was published in March 1997

- require colleges to specify how wider community involvement in planning is to be achieved.

Establishing the Market Place

The steady introduction of competition into post-16 education has been a feature of policy in recent years. The establishment of the Manpower Services Commission, the creation of training and enterprise councils (TECs) and the spread of national vocational qualifications have all contributed to an increase in the number of private training providers. Comprehensive national data about their contribution to further education are not available.

In 1993, the creation of the new college sector introduced a significantly greater element of competition between post-16 providers. Government set ambitious targets for the new sector to increase student numbers and achieve efficiency gains. The Council applied its funding arrangements to achieve these targets. Those institutions in the new sector which achieved growth and became more efficient were rewarded; those which did not were penalised. Provider competition has been fierce, particularly for full-time 16 to 19 year olds. There has been competition between colleges within the sector, as well as between the college sector, schools and providers of youth training and modern apprenticeships. The introduction of performance-related funding has been an important element in increasing competition. Colleges and training providers now need to pay as much attention to the retention and achievement of learners as they do to recruitment.

Competition has been extended by an increase in the number and range of funds allocated through a bidding process. This acceleration of competition was seen by government as pivotal in achieving its key aims for further education and training: to increase participation and levels of achievement to meet the national targets, and to increase efficiency.

Benefits for Learners

The combination of growth targets and performance-related funding has had many beneficial effects for learners. Extension of the curriculum has increased choice. Significant improvements in student services and learning support have been made. Information and guidance services have been developed to help learners to make informed programme choices and reduce the chances of dropping-out. Personal tutorial and counselling services are now more widely available. The college sector has used its new financial freedom to improve significantly the quality of the learning environment and to upgrade equipment and facilities.

On the other side of the coin, there is evidence of potential learners being denied full access to information about the choices and routes available to them, and of wasteful duplication of effort. We have heard of some schools with sixth forms refusing access to other providers at school-based careers events. Similarly, we have heard of neighbouring colleges allocating large sums of money to support marketing strategies designed solely to influence students to attend one college as opposed to another. The priority for some providers has been to improve their market share rather than to expand the market for learning. We are concerned that this response to competition wastes scarce resources and inhibits the collaboration needed to reach and engage all groups of potential learners.

Bidding competitively for funds has, in some cases, resulted in further education providers devising imaginative schemes for extending and enhancing delivery. There are examples of successful initiatives built on good and lasting partnerships. Equally, the further education landscape is littered with examples of short-term initiatives which show little evidence of coherence with mainstream developments; and often stop abruptly once the funds expire.

Identifying and Addressing Need

Rather than competing for a small part of the market, further education needs to expand the learning market as a whole. Within the college sector there are impressive examples of responses achieved by systematically mapping learning needs and drawing up profiles of local communities. Much could be achieved if these approaches were to become more widespread. In order to carry thinking forward, we commissioned jointly with the Council's learning difficulties and/or disabilities committee, a practical guide, *Identifying and Addressing Needs*. The Council published this guide in March 1997. We hope that the guide will give increased priority to this issue. The Council should adapt its guidance on preparing strategic plans to reflect the guide.

We are convinced that a national system of relatively autonomous providers, steered only by national arrangements, cannot adequately identify and achieve strategic goals at the local level. The priorities for widening participation will vary from area to area depending on, for example, social and economic structures, employment prospects and the ethnic profile. Single providers alone will not be able to deliver the specific actions required to widen participation at local level. It will need a coherent and consistent response from all local stakeholders, and this will require the establishment of a strategic focus at local level to bring harmony between the rigours of the market place – choice, quality and competition – and the public good.

Collaboration at Local Level

The introduction of independence for providers has been accompanied by increased requirements for consultation and more rigorous measurement and monitoring of performance. The Council advises colleges to share plans for provision of full-time education for 16 to 18 year olds with local education authorities. Colleges are required to consult with TECs and to obtain their agreement to their strategic plans. TECs are responsible for promoting the achievement of the national targets and, as part of this responsibility, they are expected to convene inter-agency forums which include the key providers of further education and LEAs. This emphasis on increased consultation and partnership applies equally in the realm of bidding for funds. Organisations are generally expected to consult employers and the community in preparing their bids. Some require, in addition, that bids be made on an inter-agency or partnership basis.

Many of the key local stakeholders in post-16 education and training therefore meet repeatedly in different forums to discuss similar and linked issues. Equally, many work together to deliver specific initiatives. We are concerned that this flowering of consultation, partnership and inter-agency network is often focused on single issue activities and masks the absence of any fully effective local strategic dimension in determining the character of, and priorities for, public investment in further education. The absence of a strategic dimension at local level, in our view, is a major weakness in the system which significantly reduces the potential for widening participation.

While acknowledging that the rich diversity of provision, providers and delivery mechanisms within further education must be recognised and celebrated, the diversity in arrangements for collecting data and monitoring performance, which are so crucial to planning, are its Achilles' heel. The potential for collaborative approaches at local level to prioritise needs and to facilitate coherent responses would be greatly increased if government adopted a more consistent approach to collecting data, assessing quality and monitoring performance.

We have no desire to see a return to the centralised and bureaucratic planning approaches of the past. We would wish to see local strategy emerging, developing and being sustained by partnership approaches, involving all key stakeholders, which recognise both the independence and inter-dependence of partners. The aim of these partnerships would be to promote learning and to improve the sharing of information, in order to produce local targets for widening participation. Shared information and shared analysis would enable partnerships to move on to identify and agree strategies for effectively engaging with potential learners who remain outside the system.

Sound planning requires comprehensive data of good quality. A collaborative approach to the collection of and interpretation of data is an important first step in building up the best possible picture of local participation. Between them, stakeholders in a locality possess a rich supply of local knowledge. The stimulation of debate between stakeholders, based on shared information, will provide a strong foundation for building partnerships at a strategic level.

The production of participation plans setting out agreed local targets for widening participation in support of the extended learning targets for participation advocated elsewhere in this report, will assist individual partners in their own organisational planning. In addition, by assessing the contribution towards local targets planned by each partner, the partnership would be able to identify any gaps or shortfalls. Once identified, gaps or shortfalls might be addressed by bidding for funds or through collaborative action by partnership members.

Potentially, the strategic partnerships of key stakeholders within a locality will be powerful and influential. We envisage that they would provide energy and direction within post-16 learning and be the powerhouse behind efforts to encourage new approaches and initiatives such as the establishment of the employer-based learning centres and employee development schemes which are advocated in the introduction and elsewhere in this report. They will need to bring vision and imagination to generate and support collaborative ventures which engage with those who are not economically active or not involved in learning.

It is in the interest of all stakeholders to promote the value and benefits of learning. The examples of collaboration which take place all over the country during 'Adult Learners' Week' each year, clearly demonstrated to us the potential of collaborative efforts to raise the profile of learning. We envisage the strategic partnerships playing a key role in ensuring an ongoing profile for learning supported by information and guidance in the local area.

Clearly good practice needs to mean good business, and changes in the funding arrangements which reward successful collaboration will be required.

The need for a local strategic focus is so important that we have obtained the Council's agreement to establish between 10 and 16 pilot participation partnerships across the country. During the pilot phase, activity will concentrate on the 18 plus age group.

We would anticipate eventually the creation of a national network of permanent partnerships covering all post-16 learners and learning, closely linked to the Council's regional committees, which are responsible for securing the adequacy and sufficiency of further education. In recent months, calls for partnership approaches in learning have grown to a clamour across the learning scene. In our view, the strategic participation partnerships we advocate would provide an overarching forum which could absorb many of the activities currently undertaken by the plethora of partnerships currently operating. They would therefore, reduce duplication and waste and offer coherent mechanisms for co-operation and collaboration across further education.

Community Involvement in the College Sector

Independence in the college sector has been accompanied by requirements for employers' increased involvement in governance and planning. The current arrangements for TEC approval of college strategic plans present a potentially valuable mechanism for ensuring that colleges are responsive to the labour market. However, the operation of these arrangements varies across the country and a more systematic and reciprocal approach would be beneficial. Similarly, employers' interests are now firmly and systematically located in the governance structures of colleges. The majority of board members of college corporations and TECs are required to be senior business figures. Evidence suggests that most colleges have benefited from the business expertise provided by employers who are board members.

Opportunities for the wider community to influence the nature of provision within their local college tend to be more informal and ad hoc. Some colleges foster community links to support the planning and delivery of both general and specific aspects of the curriculum. Some colleges have retained local authority representation on governing bodies, on a co-option basis, and some have identified individuals who have particular links with, or positions in, the community to serve as governors. Other colleges, however, have no formal links with the community at corporation level.

If further education is to fulfil its potential in terms of social cohesion and economic prosperity, all stakeholders need to ensure wide involvement on the part of employers and members of the community. Structures and mechanisms are in place for encouraging the college sector to become more responsive to labour market needs. Formal arrangements are necessary to ensure that it can respond more effectively to the needs of the wider community. This cannot be left to chance. Both government and the Council have roles to play in the changes needed to promote the systematic development of community involvement in planning. The government, for example, should alter the articles of government for sector colleges to make community involvement a requirement. There are many successful examples of the different forms that such involvement can take. We do not wish to specify any particular one. The Council should monitor the sector's response to the new requirement.

Learning Works – widening participation in further education

4 Funding is the most important lever for change

Public investment in post-16 learning is substantial

A radical overhaul of the present arrangements is needed

Widening participation must be the key priority for public funding in post-16 learning

Summary

Public investment in post-16 learning is substantial. The responses to our call for evidence and *Pathways to Success* show widespread agreement that changes in the government's funding of further education are essential for widening participation. Some issues have already been discussed, including the introduction of common principles for funding across 16 to 19 learning[1] and the relative contributions to funding lifelong learning to come from public funds, employers and individuals.[2] However, there should be a much more radical overhaul of the present arrangements. The key priority for public funding in post-16 learning must be to widen participation.

Recommendations

The government should:

■ create a 'Learning Nation Fund' from the national lottery funds released after the millennium to achieve the quantum leap in participation in post-16 learning needed to tackle the backlog of underachievement

■ give priority in public funding within post-16 learning to general education and transferable vocational learning, including key skills, at and leading to level 3; the costs of ensuring that all can succeed to level 3 must be recognised

- create a national framework for the funding of post-16 learning; the new system should be founded on the principle of equity and it should be simple and transparent

- harmonise funding systems and funding levels across the whole of further education

- include in the common principles for the harmonised funding system incentives and recognition of the relative costs required to widen participation

- set out clearly the relative contributions to be made from the public purse, by employers and by individuals in paying for learning

- extend tax incentives to encourage private sector employers to establish employee development schemes

- ensure that education to level 3 is free for all young people, and for adults without basic skills or who are socially or economically deprived; tax relief should be extended to all learning programmes up to level 3 which are funded by individuals

- review the current range of challenge funds and specific funds to improve the coherence of funding locally and to minimise bureaucracy

- redirect the priorities of the Single Regeneration Budget towards learning

- create a 'Learning Regeneration Fund' to provide incentives and reward for the permanent local strategic partnerships we recommend should be set up to widen participation.

What Happens Now

Public funding for further education comes from a multiplicity of different sources. The Further Education Funding Council gets the largest amount; its overall budget in 1996-97 was £3.15 billion.[3] TEC budgets in the same year were £1.4 billion, £1.19 of which were for training.[4] Funding for school sixth forms and non-schedule 2 further education provision comes to local education authorities through the 'Revenue Support Grant' for local government. The Funding Agency for Schools supports grant-maintained school sixth forms. Budget planning, funding processes, allocation systems and accountability arrangements are different for each route.

The Further Education Funding Council

The government funds the Council to support the statutory responsibilities for sufficient and adequate further education described in the *Further and Higher Education Act 1992*. The further education sector is expected to meet both demand from students and the needs of the labour market. The Council funds the strategic plans of colleges, higher education institutions, and other local learning providers, mainly local education authorities. The Council distributes funds on a national basis through a formula which has been applied to achieve government targets for growth and efficiency and to promote quality. The Council is, through its convergence policy, bringing closer together the widely varying inherited funding levels in the further education sector. Until 1997-98, an unlimited part of the budget known as the 'demand-led element' rewarded those colleges which grew faster than planned. This funding has now been withdrawn. No financial support for learners is included in Council funding; the access funds which allow colleges to help students who suffer financial hardship and the bursaries for students at residential colleges are distributed separately.

Training and Enterprise Councils

The government contracts with TECs to deliver a wide range of local services. TEC budgets cover five main areas: economic development partnerships; foundation learning; lifelong learning; business support services and business training; and employment and unemployment.

Funds for Training

The majority of TEC funding is for training: for young people through 'Youth Training' and 'Modern Apprenticeships'; and for adults through 'Training for Work'. There are a number of steps in the funding process. The Department for Education and Employment distributes funds to the 10

Government Offices; each Government Office negotiates funding with individual TECs; TECs then agree their own funding arrangements with a range of training providers. These may include colleges, private training providers, voluntary bodies and employers. Funding is usually based on a combination of the numbers of trainees at the start of programmes and the numbers gaining qualifications or jobs. The budget includes some contribution to trainees allowances for living expenses, childcare and transport costs. However, the employer pays the whole of the training allowance for around 80 per cent of young people.

Other TEC funds

TECs are also responsible for competitiveness and development funds for colleges. These funds are to encourage flexible responses to the needs of employers and the labour market; the funds will total £16 million in 1997-98. The competitiveness fund goes to colleges whose bids for capital to fund responsiveness are supported by regional groups of TECs and members of the Council's regional committees. The development fund can be used by each TEC to support competitiveness fund projects or to fund other college projects to increase flexibility and responsiveness.

TECs are funded to promote local competitiveness and the development of business skills, for example through the Investors in People scheme. They also receive funding to promote the development of lifelong learning and links between education and business in their areas.

Funding for Schools and Local Education Authorities

Each year, the government assesses the amount each LEA would need to spend on post-16 education to provide a common standard of service. However, each LEA is free to decide its own expenditure priorities and, within government limits, its council tax levels. Maintained school sixth forms are funded by LEAs under their own local schemes. The Funding Agency for Schools funds grant-maintained school sixth forms either through their former LEA's scheme or a common funding formula. The funding for LEAs' statutory responsibilities for adequate non-schedule 2 further education provision is included in the annual assessment.

Specific and Targeted Funding

Colleges, TECs and LEAs also receive funding through the regionally-based 'Single Regeneration Budget', other challenge funds, central initiatives and a range of funds from Europe. Colleges forecast an income of £78 million from European funds and £14.1 million from other grants in 1996-97.[5] Funding from the national lottery has already contributed to new college buildings. In 1997, the New Opportunities, New Choices programme will provide £160 million from the lottery for voluntary organisations promoting informal learning amongst those groups most disadvantaged in society.

The Case for Change

Complexity and Inconsistency

Each of the funding routes has been developed for separate policy objectives. We found that the bewildering variety of complex systems, the interaction between them and the plethora of specific and challenge funding presented real problems. Such funding arrangements inhibit informed debate and absorb disproportionate costs and management time. The extract that follows taken from the 1996-97 funding guidance on youth credits is a good illustration.

'A young person cannot both be receiving full-time education and have left it'

"A young person cannot at the same time receive both the fee remission entitlements associated with full-time education and be using their Youth Credit. It is not permitted, where a young person is in receipt of Youth Credits funding, for a College to claim FEFC funding other than as described in this document, and certainly not for 450 guided learning hours or more. Such a young person, who is eligible for a Youth Credit, is expected to be Youth Credits funded when attending college, except when undertaking any element of study which the TEC has said it will not fund.[6]"

The wealth of specifically-funded initiatives, with their associated jargon and acronyms have often created a confusing picture for employers.[7] These complexities must be reduced.

The costs of learning and financial support for learners are not treated consistently. The Council is not funded to give financial support for learners. However, many European funds include trainee allowances, and TEC funds include a contribution towards these in the case of some trainees. Differing arrangements mean there is little agreed evidence on which to assess equity for learners or the fairness of competition between providers. The costs, quality, outcomes and value for money associated with the diverse range of learning opportunities on offer in further education cannot easily be measured on a consistent basis.[8] The country needs to know that it is getting value for money from public funds. Funding, quality and performance measurement systems must be harmonised.

Inhibiting Lasting Partnership

Local collaboration holds the key to success in widening participation. We are agreed that the differences and inconsistencies in funding arrangements reinforce division rather than promote partnership. Analysis of the public funding for the main full-time education and training routes for 16 to 19 year olds shows that funding levels for providers vary as much within funding routes as between them. This can lead to significant differences in the resources allocated to providers at the local level. These differences can get in the way of effective collaboration.

The arrangements for specific and challenge funding are a particular concern. Evidence from the evaluation of strategies used by TECs to promote lifelong learning[9] indicates that many organisations and individuals have an interest and expertise in these activities. There is need for a greater emphasis on developing long-term relationships rather than the short-term relationships associated with the delivery of individual projects. Widening participation will take time. It is essential that there is an approach to specific and challenge funding which supports the development of lasting partnerships, achieves coherence locally and minimises bureaucracy. There should be a much greater emphasis on the role of learning in economic and social regeneration; in particular in determining the priorities for the Single Regeneration Budget. A 'Learning Regeneration Fund' should also be created at regional and subregional levels.

Mainstream Funding Needs to be Directed to Widen Participation

One of the reasons why progress in widening participation is so patchy is that it is dependent on short-term, rather than mainstream, funding. All mainstream funding systems include some recognition of the additional costs involved in providing for those with learning difficulties and/or disabilities or those with special learning needs, in particular the need to acquire basic skills. Each system also has some steers towards widening participation. For example, the Council provides additional funding to compensate institutions which remit fees for certain low income groups; TEC funding must be used to guarantee offers of training for young people not in full-time education or work; and the pre-vocational group have priority in the 'Training for Work' programme. However, more needs to be done to design mainstream funding systems which have clear systematic incentives to widen participation. Evidence about successful learning by under-represented groups should be used to develop these new systems.

Inconsistent Approaches to Public Funding for Learning by Employees

We are clear that the use of public funds for franchising – we prefer this term rather than the Council's phrase 'off-site or outward collaborative provision' – opens up new opportunities for learning and learners. However, the development of franchising has been accompanied by a heated debate, a major component of which is the argument about 'who pays' for learning for those in employment. The development of franchising has exposed inconsistencies in government policy on public funding to support learning for people in work. There is a long tradition of public funding being used to support the provision of further education and training leading to nationally-recognised qualifications for employees of all ages. Some employees pay for their own learning and use their own time; others are supported by their employers and learn in their employers' time. Council funding assumes that the contribution by employers or individuals to the costs is 25 per cent. Although TECs promote training by employers for their employees over the age of 25, government policy is that the training activity itself should not be funded. These inconsistencies must be resolved.

Learning should continue to be free for all young people and for those without basic skills. Any learning entitlement for young people must include a corresponding entitlement to free tuition. Individuals, particularly those who have done well from previous public investment in learning, and who can afford to pay more than they currently do, should be expected to do so. Public subsidy should be aimed at those who have not yet reached level 3. In general, employers should be expected to pay more than they do now. Both public funding and the taxation system should support and encourage private sector employers who formally commit themselves to the development of transferable skills in the whole of their workforce. Tax incentives should be used to stimulate the spread of employee development schemes. Tax relief should be available for any learning programme funded by individuals which is designed to raise their attainment to the level 3 entitlement.

Inequity

The inequity of the current arrangements is the most compelling reason for change. Those who have already succeeded are now most likely to take part in further learning. The successful take priority for public funding with funding skewed towards the minority who are already high achievers. Information on comparative costs for 16 to 19 year olds in 1995-96[10] show the GCSE attainments and public funding costs of young people entering schools, sector colleges and youth training. Schools recruit the best qualified young people (70 per cent have four or more GCSEs at grade C or above) and get the most funding. Colleges (where 50 per cent of students have four or more GCSEs at grade C or above) come next. Youth Training where almost 60 per cent have no GCSEs at grade C or above, and 10 per cent have no grades at all, comes third.

The principle of equity should apply across post-16 funding. Levels of funding as well as funding systems should be harmonised. All students and providers should be entitled to a fair share of funding based on common principles. Equity does not mean uniformity. Funding principles would need to take account of students' needs and the circumstances of the providers. Differences should be soundly based and transparent. Funding differences for providers would need to be carefully justified, for example, on grounds of higher costs. The system should aim to deliver common outcomes for all. Implementing these principles will take time and sensitive management. Bringing about change would challenge the freedom of local education authorities to set their own funding levels for school sixth forms. We are agreed, however, that the overwhelming national priority should be the creation of an equitable funding system.

Resourcing Widening Participation

Demand for learning is growing apace. Further education already provides successful learning experience for some of those who are under-represented. However, the capacity of the publicly-funded further education system to grow to meet increased demands is limited. The end of the demand-led element for the college sector from 1997-98 means that institutions funded by the Council can no longer receive extra funds for expansion over and above the student numbers agreed for funding. TEC budgets are capped and additional funding is not normally available for those who exceed their targets. LEA budgets too, are under pressure.

We fear that the continuing year-on-year reductions in unit costs across publicly-funded further education are providing a disincentive for providers to invest in the additional support known to be required for success with some learner groups. We are concerned that strategic management of publicly-funded further education providers is being forced to divert too much of its energy into cost-cutting when it should be attacking unaddressed need.

Resources are required both for new students and for the additional support, guidance and enrichment that under-represented groups need if more are to participate successfully in education and training. Investment is required in curriculum, institutional and technological change. Staff development is a particular concern. Redistribution of resources both to further education and within it is required if widening participation is to become a reality.

A Quantum Leap is Needed

The nation has a clear choice about the pace of change. Traditionally, we approach these matters cautiously; the redistribution of resources is determined by the acceptability of the pace of change to those from whom the funds are being redirected. Another approach is the quantum leap; a sustained and massive investment in tackling the national backlog of underachievement in the population to create a self-perpetuating learning society; by the adoption of new and demanding targets, the creation of demand, investment in new technology; and through reward and incentives for those who commit themselves to the endeavour. We believe that the funds from the national lottery, currently directed to millennium projects, should be earmarked at the start of the new century to achieve this quantum leap. A 'Learning Nation Fund' should be created. Research has shown that the people most likely to buy national lottery tickets are the less well-off, who are also likely to be those who would benefit from the chance to improve their knowledge, skills and employability. There could be no better way to re-invest their money.

Endnotes

1 DfEE, *Learning to Compete: Education and Training for 14 –19 year olds*, CM 3486, The Stationery Office, London, 1996

2 *Lifetime Learning: A Policy Framework*, DfEE, 1996

3 *The Further Education Funding Council for England*, report by the Comptroller and Auditor General, National Audit Office, February 1997

4 Response by James Paice to a parliamentary question in Hansard, 17 October 1996

5 FEFC analysis of college financial forecasts

6 DfEE, TEC National Council and FEFC, *Youth Credits and FEFC Funding*, FEFC, Coventry, 1996

7 Sue Rawlinson and Helen Connor, Developing Responsiveness: College – employer interaction Summary Report 300, Institute for Employment Studies, Falmer, 1996

8 Funding 16–19 Education and Training: Towards convergence, DfEE, 1996

9 *Evaluation of TEC lifetime learning strategies*, Institute for Employment Studies, Falmer, 1997

10 *The Public Funding Costs of Education and Training for 16–19 year olds in England 1995-96*, DfEE, March 1997

5 The Council should develop its funding arrangements to widen participation

Council funds influence the lives of millions of people

Changes in the distribution of funds are needed

Changes in the funding system must be planned to take into account the strategies needed to widen participation in future

Summary

The way the Council distributes its funds affects the lives of millions of people and their families. There were over three million learners in the further education sector in 1995-96.[1] It was the largest provider for 16 to 18 year olds in 1994-95.[2] However, the younger age group was less than a third of the overall number of students. Over two thirds were adults; most of whom were studying part time.[3] The further education funded by the Council provides over half the overall supply of intermediate skills to the economy; more than employers and the TECs provide together.[4] Demand for learning is increasing rapidly. We found a consensus that changes in the distribution of funds should be made, to provide incentives for and to recognise the costs of, drawing under-represented groups into learning and making sure that they succeed and progress. The end of extra funding for additional growth in Council activity means urgent action is essential. Changes in the funding system must be planned to take into account the other strategies required to widen participation. We welcome the Council's agreement to fund our proposal for local partnerships in 1997-98 as a sign of its commitment to widening participation.

Recommendations

The Council should in the short term:

▪ contribute more to the education and training of poorly-qualified young people by awarding entry units in inverse proportion to students' previous level of achievement

▪ contribute more to the education and training of the most needy adults by awarding entry units on the basis of relative levels of social and economic deprivation, using postcodes

▪ contribute more to the additional support and guidance of these learners through increased on-programme and achievement units or by enhanced funding for the accreditation of learner support and guidance in the *New Learning Pathway*

▪ ensure that its funding arrangements can accommodate interim achievement and unitisation of the curriculum

▪ include non-schedule 2 provision which is specifically designed to achieve progression to schedule 2(d) courses

▪ change the tariff so that employers and individuals who can afford to pay a higher proportion of the costs of their learning do so

▪ encourage methods of delivery, including franchising, which encourage participation by under-represented groups

▪ take steps to ensure the convergence policy does not impede the efforts of those in the further education sector to widen participation

▪ give priority to encourage the recording of previous educational achievement for all learners within the ISR and take account of it in the funding system

▪ extend the funding of strategic partnerships beyond 1997-98

▪ publish a 'plain English' guide showing how the funding arrangements can be used to support widening participation, in particular, the way in which additional support can be claimed.

In the longer term the Council should:

- take success in widening participation into account in the criteria for allocating any funding above the core

- aim to simplify the funding system

- develop its funding arrangements to support the increasing use of information technology, telematics, distance, open and flexible learning

- use their funding to reward institutions working in partnerships to widen participation.

Training and enterprise councils should:

- consider introducing similar rewards for those we recommend to the Council for funding work-based routes through training providers.

What Happens Now

The Council's Funding System

The Council has developed a new way of allocating funds, which operated for the first time in 1994-95. The system broke new ground because it was specifically designed to promote learning. People in the further education sector refer to it as 'the new funding methodology'. Institutions accumulate units at the three key stages of a student's learning programme: entry, on-programme and achievement. This contrasts with the previous method of funding which was based on student numbers at the start of the teaching year. The Council's system recognises the costs of different programmes. It also takes into account the need to provide free tuition and additional support for some students. There is some support for childcare costs, but it is currently restricted to students who get free tuition.

The National Audit Office found the funding methodology has been successful. It has encouraged colleges to achieve government targets for growth and efficiency. It is seen by colleges as an incentive to improve retention and achievement. Colleges also credit the funding methodology with other benefits, such as stability, an aid to planning, freedom to pursue business opportunities such as franchising, and marketing.[5] The methodology has contributed significantly to the common principles that may be developed for the funding of all 16 to 19 education and training.[6] The first stage of a fundamental review of the new funding arrangements has recently been completed. The second stage is about to start.

The principle of widening participation has been recognised in the development of the new methodology. It was argued that the recruitment of some under-represented groups could involve significantly higher costs, for example in outreach activities and that these costs would be likely to act as a disincentive to institutions if they could meet their targets by recruiting other students. One way of supporting a policy to widen access would be to neutralise such disincentives through the funding mechanism, or alternatively, to provide incentives for recruiting such students.[7] Following consultation, the principle of allocating increased entry units to under-represented groups was widely accepted.[8] A major reason for establishing the widening participation committee was the need for a body to advise on the identification of these groups and to make recommendations to the Council on how it should change its funding arrangements to encourage them to enter and succeed in further education.

Challenges to the New Arrangements

The National Audit Office's enthusiasm for the Council's funding arrangements is not universal. Many responses to the call for evidence, including some which were widely distributed,[9] raised significant challenges. Widening participation was a particular issue. Changes were needed to encourage wider participation. We were also told by some contributors that aspects of the arrangements threatened to reverse past advances.

We found early on that discussion of the funding 'methodology' could not take place in isolation. The context of year-after-year of efficiency gains, the complexity of introducing the new arrangements, their application to local circumstances and the Council's policy of converging disparate funding levels nationally, were inseparable from the new funding system. As our work developed, the passions aroused by franchising and the ending of the demand-led element intensified this debate. We found a consensus that the funding arrangements could and must be changed to give a much higher priority to widening participation.

Principles

We agreed that the principles we set out for the national funding framework should also apply to the Council. This means that the Council's system must be based on the principle of equity and it should be simple and transparent. Priority for public funds should be directed towards the entitlement to general and transferable vocational education, including key skills, at or leading to level 3. Clear steers about the responsibilities of employers and individuals for funding learning should be included. Funding should support widening participation in learning.

Equity

We accept the argument that the Council's convergence policy is intended to support the equity principle. The Council inherited a system in which there were considerable disparities in funding between different areas of the country. However, the progressive implementation of the convergence policy has raised serious questions about the present assumptions underlying the calculation of student activity. We believe that the implementation of our recommendations will go a long way to answering those questions. We welcome the Council's initiative to examine costs in London. Disentangling the issues of London costs, the London weighting and the characteristics of students attending London colleges will be an important contribution to the debate. The present convergence policy may present risks to widening participation and, pending discussion of our recommendations, we are anxious that the Council develops its convergence policy to avoid these risks.

Simplicity and Transparency

While the funding system is undoubtedly simple and transparent in principle; its actual operation and administration are complex. We are particularly concerned that some institutions are more on the ball than others. Clever ways have been found of interpreting the funding guidance. Elsewhere, less imagination has been devoted to the task. Analysis of the additional support units claimed by colleges shows wide variation in practice. Funding for widening participation should be a matter of right; not dependent on providers' imagination. The Council should set out clearly and accessibly how those seeking to widen participation can legitimately use its funding to do so.

Funding Priorities

The priority for public funding should be for all to have an entitlement to achieve level 3. We are concerned that, in the drive for growth, some of the funding which should have been directed towards widening participation may have been diverted to individuals who could have afforded to pay more, to employers, and to the achievement of qualifications which are of doubtful long-term value. Funding should clearly be directed in line with the priorities set out in this report.

Funding to Support Widening Participation

Funding should support successful learning. The characteristics of good practice provide a framework for the key issues that should influence the design of funding systems for widening participation. Guidance, curriculum enrichment and support have been shown to make a real difference to successful learning for those with low levels of previous achievement. The need to recognise small steps in learning, in particular for adults, and progression from non-schedule 2 to schedule 2 provision are crucial. Encouraging partnership and collaboration is also essential.

The Learners

There are two ways of identifying groups which are under-represented in colleges and more generally in post-16 learning. One way is to look at specific groups by age, sex, race, or ethnicity; however, the representation of these groups in learning nationally changes over time and there are different patterns of participation in different communities. This approach is therefore not suitable to identify under-represented groups for funding. The other method is to identify more general characteristics such as previous educational achievement, income level and where people live. We found these characteristics apply both nationally and locally and stand the test of time.

Not all under-represented groups cost more to educate and train. Much can be achieved within existing funding by responding to learners' needs with imagination. We have seen participation widened by providing better information, removing entry barriers, providing the right curriculum and qualifications, delivering learning support and involving community groups and employers.

Some groups of learners, however, are more difficult to recruit, more likely to drop out and less likely to achieve at all stages of their learning. Previous educational achievement is the key for 16 year olds. Those with high attainment at GCSE stay on in education and do so for longer. Adults least likely to participate are those who left school early, and have no recent experience of learning.

The college sector is already recruiting students with a wide range of prior attainment. Under half of the 16 year olds entering general further education and tertiary colleges have already achieved foundation target 1 (equivalent to five GCSEs at grade C or above), whereas three quarters of 16 year old students attending sixth form colleges have already reached this target. Analysis of Council data confirms that there are many 16 year old students in sector colleges who have some GCSEs but who have not yet reached foundation target 1. However, those with the worst GCSE results are less likely to participate.[10]

Students with low levels of prior attainment are more likely to be poor and to live in economically and socially disadvantaged areas. Council data show links between poor levels of retention and achievement, low income, and living in areas of social and economic disadvantage. Retention rates for adult students on benefit are on average 9 per cent lower than for other adult students and their achievement rates are lower by a similar amount. Evidence shows that the provision of additional support, guidance and curriculum enrichment for these students makes a difference to retention, achievement and progression.[11]

Demand for learning is increasing and will continue to do so in future. Pressures to reduce costs and improve performance are also unrelenting. Funding arrangements must recognise the costs of the additional work required to ensure that these students are not left by the wayside. The students must be 'unit-rich', so that institutions have clear incentives to recruit them and to ensure that they succeed and progress. The ending of the funding for extra growth in Council activity means urgent action is essential.

Identifying Under-represented Learners in the Funding Methodology

Any changes to funding should be linked to the characteristics of students, not to the characteristics of the institution. We assessed three options for identifying students:

- previous educational achievement
- income level as indicated by their entitlement to benefit
- the social and economic characteristics of where students lived.

We looked at the evidence relating to each of these options. We examined the practicalities for speedy implementation. We tested our conclusions with a group of practitioners. We concluded that the best way of identifying students was by their previous educational achievement. At present, the only group for which the data are good enough is the 16 to 19 year old group. The Council should work with institutions to improve the quality of these data over time. The Universities and Colleges Admission Service, on behalf of the government, is developing the new database for lifelong learning, known as 'Profile', which will serve as the electronic transcript of the relaunched 'National Record of Achievement' or 'Progress File', and this may well improve the availability and quality of these data on achievements in the future. The use of postcodes linked to an index of social conditions should be used for older age groups where data on previous educational achievement are currently inadequate. This approach will not pinpoint everyone, but it is the best of the available options. It will identify pockets of rural poverty as well as larger areas of urban deprivation. There may be continuing difficulties in assessing the relevance of adults' previous experience and qualifications. We concluded that funding must support learners not just at the entry stage but throughout their learning programmes. We also acknowledged that to avoid devaluing the unit of funding our proposals incorporate reduced units for some learners at the same time as those for others are increased.

Other Changes

A number of other short-term and long-term changes to support widening participation include strategic partnerships, the introduction of the 'New Learning Pathway', the development of a national credit framework, the 'University for Industry', and an increasing role for information technology in learning. Given the long time-scales for the introduction of changes to the funding arrangements, it is important that the Council takes a long-term view and plans well in advance for their implementation. We welcome the Council's agreement to fund our proposal for local partnerships to widen participation in 1997-98 as a sign of its commitment to widening participation. The responses to the consultation document were positive. A significant number of respondents pointed out the need for a longer-term commitment of funding if lasting changes are to be brought about. We hope that the Council will be able to extend the funding of partnerships well beyond 1997-98.

Endnotes

1   FEFC press release, Student Numbers, Retention, Achievements and Destinations at Colleges in the Further Education Sector in England in 1995-96

2   Skills for 2000: Supplement to the report on progress towards the national targets for education and training, National Advisory Council for Education and Training Targets, London, 1996

3   FEFC press release, Student Numbers, Retention, Achievements and Destinations at Colleges in the Further Education Sector in England in 1995-96

4   *Skill supply and further education – A paper from the DfEE, FEFC and TEC National Council Statistics Working Group*, December 1996

5   *The Further Education Funding Council for England*, report by the Comptroller and Auditor General, National Audit Office, February 1997

6   DfEE, *Learning to Compete: Education and Training for 14–19 year olds*, CM 3486, London, 1996

7   FEFC, *Funding Learning*, FEFC, Coventry, 1992

8   Circular 93/32 *Recurrent Funding Methodology: Tariff Values for 1994-95*, FEFC, November 1993

9   The monograph *Lewisham not Lewes* produced by Lewisham College in September 1995 which the committee followed up by a visit to the college on 26 January 1996

Tony Uden, *Widening Participation: Routes to a learning society:* A policy discussion paper, NIACE, Leicester, 1996. Chapter 4, The Place of the Funding Methodology and the Challenge to the Kennedy Committee, includes a useful summary of many of the points raised elsewhere together with some proposed modifications to the funding arrangements.

Hilary Steedman and Andy Green, Widening Participation in Further Education and Training: A survey of the issues, Centre for Economic Performance, 1996

10 Council statistical evidence commissioned by the committee

11 Council statistical evidence commissioned by the committee

6 New systems of financial support for students must be created

Financial and practical support for learners is crucial for widening participation

The present system is neither fair nor transparent; a root and branch review is needed

Some changes must be made immediately

Summary

Financial and practical support for learners is crucial for widening participation. Barriers, such as family and childcare commitments, costs and transport are clearly identified in a 1996 survey of the most important reasons for adults not participating in learning.[1] Financial hardship is also a factor in drop-out.[2] Many of the people in the groups which need to be engaged more widely in learning have low incomes. Our call for evidence was dominated by responses about the ways in which the current arrangements create barriers for learners. We have concluded that the present system of support for post-16 learning is neither fair nor transparent. A root and branch review is needed. Some changes must be made immediately.

Recommendations

The government should:

■ undertake a major review of financial support for further education students

- ensure that principles of fairness and transparency apply to financial support for learners throughout post-16 education

- increase significantly access funds for the college sector and remove the current restrictions on eligibility until the review is complete

- give priority within the public funding which is available for financial support to students to increase the numbers of people aiming to achieve level 3

- consider fully the implications for widening participation of any detailed proposals for individual learning accounts

- evaluate the impact of the Job-Seeker's Allowance, and recognise the contribution that achieving qualifications can make to individuals seeking, securing and retaining jobs.

The Council should:

- add the funds currently provided through the funding allocation for childcare to access funds to create a new 'Access and Childcare fund'

- incorporate a measure of 'need' in the formula for the distribution of the new fund.

What Happens Now

Employers are the most significant providers of funding for learning.[3] However, employed people with little previous achievement or qualifications are the least likely to have access to employer-sponsored education and training. The availability of financial and practical support for young people who have not started work, people who are unlikely to be supported by their employers, and those who are not in work, is particularly important for widening participation.

The costs to the public purse of participating in learning in further education are modest. Most learners live and study locally. Individual learners needs vary. They may have to pay for course and examination fees, books, equipment, transport and, for some, the costs of caring for children and other dependent relatives, and living expenses. There is evidence that some of the costs of participating in further education have risen. Travel costs are a problem for all students. Access to information technology is becoming more important than ever. The average annual value of a local authority discretionary award in 1994-95 was £665.[4] However, some learners have a struggle to find the small amounts of funding they need.

Some of the problems

The National Union of Students told us how unexpected expenses could upset tightly planned budgets. There is evidence that only more experienced learners considered the hidden costs of learning such as books, photocopying and stationery before enrolling.[5] Students at Lewisham College told us how having to buy even a computer disk could present problems. The level of financial support for adult students was high on the list of issues the students at the Northern College for Residential Adult Education wanted to discuss.

Financial support for learning in further education comes from a bewildering variety of sources. We looked at the main ones.

Fees

Fees for further education are decided by a mixture of national and local policies. All young people in school sixth forms and those in colleges who are under 19 at the time of starting their courses, receive free tuition. TEC-funded programmes for young people and adults are free. Institutions in the college sector decide their own fee policies. If they provide free tuition for adults who receive means-tested benefits and their dependants, and for students on basic education courses, they receive compensating funding. We were told that because this policy was linked to benefit, it did not take account of others not able to pay full fees, in particular, part-time and low-paid workers. Many in the college sector are choosing to forgo fees for more students than those covered by the funding policy. It is not clear whether this strategy is aimed at adult students on low incomes, or a more general approach to marketing. Tax relief at source for vocational training leading to NVQs can reduce the actual cost for individuals who pay their own fees.

Discretionary Awards

Discretionary awards made by local education authorities are the main plank of government policy explicitly aimed at meeting the costs of students learning in colleges. Some authorities make hardly any discretionary awards and only one in twenty students receives them. The amount an individual receives and what it covers varies enormously from one local education authority area to another. Some students, despite their financial need, do not receive an award at all. Expenditure on discretionary awards fell by a third between 1992-93 and 1994-95.[6] By 1996-97, it is estimated that expenditure will have halved.[7] Students' chances of getting awards depend on where they live or what they study, rather than on need or merit.

Training Allowances

TEC-funded programmes offer financial support for some trainees. Some young people on Youth Training programmes receive financial support with transport and other learning costs. They also receive a training allowance which, as a minimum, is the equivalent of income support. Some TECs may receive contributions from employers and pay more. Unemployed adults on 'Training for Work' programmes get their social security benefits plus a £10 top-up. Transport and other costs associated with the learning programme are met.

Access Funds

Access funds allow colleges to help alleviate the financial hardship of participating in full-time further and higher education students over the age of 19. The college sector will get just over £6 million for access funds in 1997-98. The last time the funds increased was in 1995-96. In 1995-96, 53,000 students applied for access funds. Just under 47,000 (less than 2 per cent of all students) were successful. Each student received on average £132 for fees, books and equipment, transport, childcare and accommodation.[8] Colleges told us that access funds were essential for responding sensitively and flexibly to student hardship.

Using access funds flexibly

On the basis of detailed research into retention, Manchester College of Arts and Technology uses a substantial proportion of its access fund as a travel allowance. The allowance is paid retrospectively at the end of each term on the basis of a 75 per cent minimum attendance. The college reports this had a major impact on retention.

There is evidence that more colleges, particularly those in areas of high unemployment, are increasingly supplementing access funds and extending support to younger students. Some devote as much as 3 to 4 per cent of their annual budgets to these funds.[9] Some colleges use these funds as matching funding to get support from the European Social Fund. Colleges also help students to apply for funds from local business or charities.

Council Funding for Childcare

The vast majority of the Council's funds are devoted to funding learning itself, not to the practical support that learners need. There are two exceptions to this. One is the bursary scheme to support adult students at residential colleges; the other is childcare. Around £3 million was provided for childcare in 1995-96. Less than half of the colleges claimed any units. There is widespread dissatisfaction with the current arrangements. There are those who argue that the Council's resources should be directed solely to learning; childcare should be funded elsewhere. There are those who argue that the limited support the Council offers is both inadequate and inflexible.

Social Security Benefits

Social security benefits are an essential source of support for some students. Our research suggested that there were around 100,000 unemployed people in the college sector studying on benefit. For certain groups, such as lone parents and some people with learning difficulties and/or disabilities, who receive income support, there are no restrictions on the time that can be spent studying. The amount of time that unemployed people can devote to study is restricted. The new Job-Seeker's Allowance introduced, in October 1996, a national definition of the restriction in the college sector. Students on Council-funded courses which average 16 or fewer guided learning hours a week can continue to receive benefit provided they remain available for work and actively seek it. Unlike the previous '21-hour rule', private study time is not included in the hours counted. From April 1997, 'Workskill Pilot' schemes have been introduced in four areas of the country to test whether more flexible study rules would improve prospects of employment for unemployed people.

People who are unemployed are less likely to study than those in work. A national survey in 1995,[10] undertaken before the introduction of the new Job-Seeker's Allowance arrangements, showed that 14 per cent of respondents were studying while receiving benefit. Their characteristics reflect those in the learning population generally: more women were studying than men; study rates were found to peak among those aged 25 to 34 and were lower among those over 55; over a quarter of professionals were studying, in contrast to one in 10 of the unskilled and skilled manual workers; those who were studying while unemployed were more likely to be already qualified.

Passions run high about the interconnection between the benefits system and further education. We were told that the system was a major barrier to widening participation. It forced people to cease courses leading to worthwhile qualifications and sustained employability to take up short-term unskilled jobs; it operated inconsistently; and fear of losing benefit was a major deterrent to study.

The Case for Change

Sadly, we found there has been no comprehensive and reliable investigation in this country of the relationship between participation and student support in either further or higher education. There is an impressive body of evidence from the USA supporting the thesis that financial aid can widen participation. More research in the UK is undoubtedly needed. Our case for changing the arrangements does not have to rely on research, but rather on the evidence that the current system is riddled with anomalies and creates barriers for learning for those who need it most.

Inequity

The government has asked the National Committee of Enquiry into Higher Education to 'have regard to . . . the following principles . . . arrangements for student support should be fair and transparent . . . '[11] This principle should apply not only to higher education, but to the whole of the nation's policies with regard to financial support for students. Compared with full-time students in higher education, learners in further education are the poor relations. The 1996 *Learning to Compete* white paper set out a new learning credits entitlement for young people to enter education and training to level 3 up to the age of 21. No corresponding entitlement to financial support, even to the payment of course fees, was proposed. Discretionary awards represent a lottery rather than an entitlement. Full-time higher education students, on the other hand, are entitled to free tuition, a maintenance award based on parental or family income, and access to a non-means-tested, publicly-subsidised loan, the average value of which in 1995-96 was £1,243. The average value of the higher education maintenance award alone in 1995-96 was £1,726, two and a half times the average value of the discretionary award in further education. Further education gets about 20 per cent of the total access fund budget; the remainder goes to higher education. Five per cent of full-time students in higher education institutions received access funds in 1995-96. On average the amount they received was £358; between two and a half and three times the average of all students, including those on higher education courses, in colleges.[12]

Widening participation demands that similar support for learners in further education be considered as a matter of urgency.

Barriers to Learning

The confusion and uncertainty which surround financial support for students create significant barriers to entering and staying in learning for those whose need is greatest. The different arrangements may distort choice for those with low incomes. We were told that the entitlement to free school meals for sixth formers from families on income support or the trainee allowance on some TEC-funded programmes could influence a young person's choice of initial programme. We found that finance was one of the complex cocktail of factors which could influence a student's decision to leave a course. Student withdrawal rates in further education colleges were higher for those qualifying for income-related fee remission than for others.[13] What may be perfectly sensible and logical differences to policy-makers and those in the know may be difficult for learners to understand.

Vagaries of benefit awards

Two students attending the same college course, who are both unemployed find it difficult to understand why one of them receives a weekly benefit plus £10 as part of Training for Work whilst the other has benefit suspended because of a judgement that attending the course means the student is not actively seeking work. Word of these vagaries spread like wildfire and potential students can be deterred from engaging in learning for fear of losing benefit.

Local Decision-making

The disparities in different areas of the country, which result from the complete freedom of each local education authority to determine the level of expenditure on awards for further education students, are unacceptable. For equality to prevail, local discretion must operate within some national minimum standards. Levels of expenditure on access funds are determined on a national basis, but local discretion is used to distribute them to students. There were examples of colleges, both individually and in partnership, making imaginative use of funds. Access funds are distributed now according to the number of eligible students enrolled at each college in the previous year. The basis of the allocation could be improved if a measure of student need were included in the formula. With this proviso, access funds are a sensible and cost- effective way for colleges to accord priorities and respond to the needs of individual students in varying local circumstances. Increased funds are needed and the current eligibility criteria should be relaxed.

Childcare enables both women and men to learn; learning parents create learning families. Those in families with children, in particular one-parent families, are less committed to learning than those without children.[14] Childcare is essential if lone parents are to be encouraged to acquire the skills and qualifications for independence. There is, however, a limit to the funds the Council can devote to childcare and these limited funds have to be used in the best possible way. This could be achieved by transferring the funds currently used for childcare in the main funding allocation to access funds. Colleges would then have the discretion to meet childcare needs locally, rather than through a national formula. The new fund should be renamed the 'Access and Childcare Fund'. The Council fund for childcare should be available to young people as well as those over 19. External institutions that wished to do so should be able to apply for a share.

Learning and Social Security

The key policy imperative behind the Job-Seeker's Allowance is to get people back to work; it is not intended to fund full-time students. The argument that intensive learning and achieving qualifications enhances long-term employability is very persuasive. This is particularly the case for people on low pay and those who are unqualified who are least likely to receive training from employers. The 'Workskill Pilots' provide examples of arrangements where immediate availability for work has less priority than gaining qualifications for work. We believe that the government should review the Job-Seeker's Allowance, recognising the contributions that qualifications can make to seeking, securing and retaining jobs.

There is scope for immediate change. We are particularly concerned about the impact on 19 year olds in low-income families who are part way through full-time courses after entitlement to child benefit stops on their nineteenth birthday. Considerable public investment in their education will go to waste if they drop out. Changes must take place to ensure they can complete their qualifications. We have been assured by officials that the '16-hour rule' has replaced the previous local interpretations of part- time courses by different benefits offices. We have been told, by those on the ground, of instances where the new rules are being applied inconsistently. These problems must be put to rights.

Individual Learning Accounts

Various models of learning accounts have been proposed. The state, employers and individuals would pay money into an account for the individual to spend on education and training. There is some evidence that funding for individuals is an incentive to participate. We were therefore attracted to the idea in principle as a radical and powerful tool for creating a mass learning culture. Its potential must be investigated in depth. The introduction of any scheme, however, must be designed to take into account existing arrangements in further education. A scheme which relies heavily on contributions from employers will exclude those not in employment. Without positive support and guidance, those who are excluded – and therefore have little evidence of the benefits that accrue from learning – may have little or no incentive to use their accounts.

Endnotes

1 Campaign for Learning: Attitudes to Learning: Mori State of the Nation Poll, Summary Report, Royal Society of Arts, 1996

2 PSI research for the committee

3 Hutten & Rice, quoted in Malcolm Maguire; Chris Hasluck; Anne Green, Identifying Target Groups for Individual Commitment Policies, DfEE and The Stationery Office, 1996

4 PSI research for the committee

5 PSI research for the committee

6 PSI research for the committee

7 Chartered Institute of Public Finance and Accountancy, quoted in FE Now!, May 1997

8 PSI research for the committee

9 PSI research for the committee

10 David Bottomley, Stephen McKay and Robert Walker, Unemployment and Jobseeking: A national survey in 1995, Research Report No. 62, Department of Social Security and The Stationery Office, London, 1997

11 National Committee of Inquiry into Higher Education, Background Information Booklet, January 1997

12 PSI research for the committee

13 Council statistical evidence commissioned by the committee

14 Malcolm Maguire; Chris Hasluck; Anne Green, Identifying Target Groups for Individual Commitment Policies, DfEE and TSO, 1996

7 We know how to widen participation – now we need to make it happen

There is good practice in widening participation, but it is not systematic, consistent or equitable

The design and delivery of learning programmes must include extra help for people who have previously not succeeded

Measuring participation and achievement must include the assessment of learning gain

Summary

Knowledge and expertise already exists for reaching and supporting under-represented learners in further education. Luck, however, plays too great a role in whether the needs of a prospective learner are met. Even within individual institutions, good practice in widening participation is patchy. Good practice starts with the identification of those who do not take part. Once the learners have taken their first step, they must receive good quality information and guidance. They have to be well supported on their journey through a carefully designed learning programme and they may well need practical help to continue. The delivery of programmes must be of the highest standards. None of this can happen accidentally; it requires planning and management. Learners have to be able to recognise and record their learning gains and have them celebrated.

Recommendations

The government should:

- create a national partnership to develop a credit framework for implementation within the next five years
- commission work to develop a national system for measuring learning gain in all forms of post-16 learning
- include widening participation in the common standards for harmonised systems of quality assurance and measurement of performance across further education.

The Council should:

- play a leading role in the drive to develop a national credit framework
- support the development of the 'New Learning Pathway'
- promote the committee's good practice guide on widening participation
- recognise the urgency of improving teaching quality by issuing guidance to support the new inspection arrangements and in doing so highlight the importance of teacher development
- publish the current data on participation, enrolment, retention, achievement and progression in the sector
- provide guidance to institutions on measuring participation and establishing benchmarks and targets
- consider incorporating a widening participation element into its performance indicators for colleges when these are next reviewed.

Colleges should:

- comment on their implementation of the nine characteristics of good practice in their annual self-assessment report
- ensure that teacher development activities are aimed at training to meet the new challenges of wider participation in education.

Training and enterprise councils should:

- include further education teachers in their teacher placement targets.

We Know How to Do It

We are not starting from scratch when we aim to widen participation. The knowledge and expertise to widen participation already exists. There is much exciting and innovative practice throughout post-16 learning. What is lacking is a systematic policy to bring a wider spectrum of the population into learning. If equity is to prevail, we must remove the element of luck in whether the needs of a prospective learner are met or not.

We found many impressive examples of providers reaching out to their local communities. Under-represented groups are carefully identified, and welcomed into a rich variety of relevant learning opportunities.

Identifying target groups and measuring success

The Northern College for Residential Adult Education has a comprehensive range of performance criteria by which to judge its success in relation to widening participation: these include targets for recruitment by age, sex, social class, ethnicity, disability and previous qualifications. The college particularly targets men and women over 20 who are disadvantaged and who would benefit from a period of intensive residential study.

Using technology to support students with physical disabilities

Kingsway College has some innovative programmes for students with physical disabilities. They are taught keyboard skills and how to communicate and obtain information through the Internet. Students are lent equipment and given funds to enable them to gain access to the Internet at home. The college provides tutorial support and a telephone help-line. Some students are using this technology to investigate employment opportunities.

Encouraging Success

It is not enough to attract new learners through the door. Programmes have to be specially designed to meet the needs of people who want to make a fresh start in learning. Programmes which offer adults access to higher education provide a good example. They offer a flexible curriculum which allows such people an element of choice. Study skills and personal action-planning form an important part of the course, together with other key skills such as communications, information technology skills and in some cases, numeracy. Learners are able to collect credit for each unit studied and to build up a record of achievement which counts towards their overall qualification. If a student has to leave, it is possible for them to come back at a later date and to build on existing credits. Learners offer each other mutual support. Adults bring with them a great wealth of experience and they are encouraged to draw on this experience for their own and for others' benefit. Learners are taught the skills necessary to work in groups and on their own.

Meeting the needs of the learner

The Connections programme at Norwich City College provides accessibility and flexibility to adult students through a modular curriculum. It offers a high degree of tutorial support and encourages students to support each other. Students' confidence is built through a range of personal development modules. They also try a series of vocational taster modules to help them to decide what they would like to focus on. There is a strong emphasis on the practical aspects of the curriculum and continual assessment procedures replace traditional tests and examinations. Many students have progressed from Connections courses to other college courses. Connections graduates could be found on 81 courses in the college in 1996.

Teaching Quality

Sadly, the quality of teaching for new learners is not of universally good quality. The Council's chief inspector has reported a worsening of inspection grades on basic skills courses in the college sector. The reasons for this include the recruitment of inexperienced teachers, a lack of support for the expanding number of part-time teachers, and insufficient sharing of learning materials amongst teachers. A high proportion of classes are taught by staff who do not possess specialist qualifications in teaching basic skills or in teaching English for speakers of other languages. Engaging new learners represents a considerable challenge for teachers. Providers should recognise the importance of investing in the development and training of teachers to ensure good quality education for new learners.

There are many examples of providers encouraging and supporting learners so that they can successfully complete courses and training programmes.

Supporting learners to successfully stay the course

Knowsley Community College has tackled the problem of students who do not complete courses by instigating a cross-college retention project. The college has recognised that student withdrawal is a multi-faceted problem for which there is no single solution. It has therefore promoted action on a number of fronts: responding rapidly to non-attendance; improving the inter-personal skills of staff dealing with students with challenging behaviour; creating 'Retention Action Teams' in all curriculum areas; improving the collection of student data; and setting up a continuous review system to measure the effectiveness of the project. The college has seen considerable improvements in staying-on rates since the project started in 1994.

Many schemes have been set up to try to give practical help to learners to ease their entry into learning or to help them to continue their studies.

A supportive partnership

'Fast Forward' is a Nottinghamshire County Council initiative, designed to break down barriers which affect an individual's decision to take up education or training. Working through partnerships with local colleges and a wide range of voluntary and statutory organisations, it provides: a 'brokering role' encouraging the development of new provision in local communities; impartial advice and guidance; outreach work; and innovative projects. The initiative provides support for travel, childcare and other support costs. It supported over 3,500 students in 1996-97.

We have been impressed by the work of institutions in the sector which sometimes goes unacknowledged. These have included colleges of agriculture, and the specialist designated colleges, most notably the residential colleges. We believe that the residential colleges have the potential to play a key strategic role in widening participation. The colleges provide a distinct curriculum offer, residential learning environments which attract and support adults who would not otherwise take part in further education, and opportunities for accelerated learning through intensive study. We look forward to the outcomes of the Council's review of the funding of residential colleges.

Knowledge and Expertise Outside the College Sector

There is a wealth of knowledge and expertise outside the college sector. Good practice can be found in the services provided for adult learners and school pupils by local education authorities, by trade unions, by employers and in the activities which take place in voluntary and community groups.

The Women's Technology Scheme in Liverpool

The Women's Technology Scheme in Liverpool was established in 1983 to provide training for women in new technologies. It recruits women with few or no qualifications and aims to enable them to progress to employment in technical professions where women are traditionally under-represented. A high proportion of students gain qualifications and a significant number progress from full-time courses to more advanced study or employment.

Training within the workplace plays a vital role in widening participation. It is particularly important when the skills being acquired are transferable from job to job, reflecting the needs for a flexible and well-trained workforce. Also important are employee development schemes which are designed to raise the expectations of the workforce and to give them a positive attitude to education and training.

Ford EDAP

The key principle of the Ford motor company's Employee Development Assistance Programme is to extend access to further and higher education to people who have previously been excluded or who have excluded themselves from participation. The scheme offers all Ford employees the opportunity to participate in non-job specific adult education in their own time. It is designed to combat a key barrier to participation in continuing education for Ford employees: the three-shift system. In order to be open to all members of the workforce, the programme provides some courses on site. It also influences the nature and delivery of external adult education provision. Workers can claim up to a maximum of £200 a year to offset the costs involved in attending courses.

Unipart 'U'

Unipart 'U' is the company's university at the Group's head office in Oxford. It is an integral part of working life – employees enter through the 'U' every day on their way to and from work as well as teach in the facility. There are around 180 different courses which have been designed to be practical so that attendees 'train for work' and can apply 'this morning's learning to this afternoon's job'.

Many of the successful schemes to attract people to education and training involve partnerships and collaborative groups. Partnerships can strengthen and support individual initiatives for the benefit of the wider community. The sharing of knowledge about under-represented groups better informs all those involved. TECs can have an important strategic role to play in such partnerships. Other examples of partnership activities which have widened participation include franchise agreements between colleges and other providers such as employers, community or voluntary groups. Through these agreements a college ensures the quality of the partner's learning programme. Franchised programmes have given opportunities to people who might otherwise never have entered learning and gained qualifications.

Characteristics of Good Practice

In examining the evidence we have identified nine main characteristics of good practice in widening participation:

- marketing is planned and based on intelligence
- there are strategies for contacting non-participants
- good quality information and guidance is readily available and impartial
- there is effective support for learning
- financial and practical support is provided
- the curriculum is relevant and enables students to progress
- there is effective teaching and promotion of learning
- there are mechanisms for recording students' achievements which acknowledge all learning, are meaningful to students and are recognised by employers, education providers and others
- management information is accurate and used to evaluate students' progress and other aspects of provision.

These characteristics are more than the sum of their parts. Action to widen participation needs to be present in all aspects of the work of the college or other provider. This way, not only are people encouraged to participate, but they will be helped to stay in learning and to achieve. There were no providers in our sample to which all of the nine characteristics applied, although several were exhibiting some of the characteristics. Good practice in widening participation varied greatly from provider to provider and within organisations or establishments. If under-represented groups are to be moved from the margins to the mainstream of learning in further education, the different elements of good practice need to be seen as a whole and should underpin and drive organisational culture, strategy, structure and practice.

We intend to publish a good practice guide, based on the evidence gathered, to test these characteristics. The guide will include an analysis of the needs of the learner, the role of the provider, and a set of benchmarks for each characteristic. We hope the Council will promote the guide.

The Lottery of Learning

Access to good provision is a lottery for under-represented learners. In some areas of the country they have more and better opportunities than in others. Some communities have had their needs carefully and comprehensively mapped and identified, and some have not. By no means all providers have adopted strategies to remove barriers to learning. Some types of college are more likely to have strategies for widening participation than others. Thus, where you live becomes a very important factor in whether you will be able to participate in education and training.

Another aspect of this lottery relates to the type of learning opportunity the prospective learner requires. Many of the initiatives presented to us depend on short-term funding. When the funding runs out the initiative stops. Some learners therefore have made the first steps into education only to be thwarted early on in their journey by the removal of the finance. This is a particular problem with community initiatives. The source of funding may be an unknown quantity to learners, but it can actually be of paramount importance in determining how far they can take their studies.

Barriers to Participation

There are many barriers to participation in learning. To widen participation as many of these barriers as possible need to be removed. Although by no means all of the barriers to participation are put up by providers, they must bear the main responsibility for helping students to tackle them.

Changes that Need to be Made Now

We propose a 'New Learning Pathway' for those aged 18 and over who have low levels of attainment in education and training. Those offering the pathway will design opportunities to meet the needs of learners and to enable them to make learning gains at a level and pace suited to them. It will include opportunities for foundation, intermediate and advanced qualifications.

On the pathway, each person will have an individual learning programme, accessing the qualifications they want, at the levels they need from a menu, and explicitly building in the skills they require to continue learning. To make this work, guidance, support and recognition of life experiences are essential. Accordingly, at the heart of the pathway will be a planned programme of learning support, accredited so that its learning outcomes are recognised. This will extend the value of the pathway and help to open up progression routes. From the pathway, learners should be able to move on to a wide range of further learning opportunities.

The pathway represents a commitment and quality promise. Colleges and other providers wishing to offer it will be expected to work specifically from the needs of locally under- represented groups, and to meet challenging criteria based on our characteristics of good practice. They will be encouraged to work in partnership to make the best possible offer. We expect the pathway to open up new routes for learning, to encourage many more providers to give priority to under-represented groups, and to offer them status and recognition. The cost of the pathway, including the accredited programme of learning support, should be fully recognised in the Council's funding tariff.

A National Framework for Credit

Education and training must become much more flexible in order to meet the needs of those in under-represented groups. There should be a national framework of credit for further education, similar to that already developed in Wales and by open college networks. This framework will provide accreditation for interim achievement. Learners will be able to chart their learning gain, get recognition for their work and build up credit through their lives. The 'UCAS Profile', acting as the database of lifelong learning, will enable learners to record the credits achieved and enable them to present evidence of credit accumulation. An expansion of learning in the workplace and outside conventional institutions and progression between learning programmes and different providers will follow. The framework will help curriculum design and development, including the use of information technology. It will require funding to be available which recognises achievement at unit level. There are already local examples of credit frameworks and FEDA has provided us with one route map to develop the approach on a national basis.

Our recommendation takes account of the concerns about the development of such a framework. We do not wish to put any barriers in the way of the implementation of the recommendations of the Dearing Review of qualifications for young people. We believe that our recommendation is not inconsistent with these much-needed developments. The development of the new framework must respond to fears that a credit accumulation approach will dilute the quality and currency of some existing qualifications. In our view, the development process should also involve rigorous criteria for the review of all qualifications. There are concerns about costs, and building the new system will involve additional costs. We also believe that it would bring about some savings by rationalising the enormous number of qualifications now available. Development costs for new qualifications would also reduce.

Value-added or 'Learning Gain'

Whilst it is relatively straight forward to measure added value, or 'learning gain', from GCSE to GCE A level, it is difficult to measure the learning gain for vocational qualifications. A nationally-agreed system to measure 'learning gain' in post-16 learning is urgently required. This would provide a way of understanding and valuing all achievement. It would also help to measure progress in achieving widening participation.

National Standards for Quality Assessment and Performance Measurement

National standards for widening participation are required if participation is to be widened systematically and consistently. We welcome the Council's revised inspection framework which identifies widening participation as a key element in each institution's mission. We have developed standards to accompany the characteristics of good practice in widening participation. We think these standards should be widely shared and included in the guidance to support the new inspection arrangements based on self-assessment. These standards should include staff development.

The framework we have developed for measuring widening participation will provide those who work in the college sector with much-needed help in setting targets and measuring progress. The key elements in the framework are the monitoring of recruitment by level of prior attainment, or by postcodes where evidence of attainment is not available, and monitoring retention, achievement and progression in terms of student characteristics such as age, sex and ethnic group, as well as by prior level of attainment. We want the Council to publish the current data on participation, enrolment, retention, achievement and progression in the college sector and to provide guidance for the sector on measuring participation, establishing benchmarks and setting targets.

We considered whether we should set some sector performance indicators for widening participation, but concluded that it would be inappropriate at this stage. It is important that under-represented groups are defined at the local level by colleges or groups of providers. Definitions are likely to differ from place to place. It would therefore be difficult to construct a national performance indicator for the sector which satisfactorily summarised local initiatives and also encapsulated data on participation, retention and achievement which we believe are fundamental to widening participation. We look to the Council to consider the options for incorporating a widening participation element into its performance indicators for colleges when they are next reviewed.

We strongly support initiatives to harmonise systems of quality assessment and performance measurement across further education. We believe that widening participation should be included in these common systems.

Learning Works – widening participation in further education

8 A coherent system of information, advice and guidance is essential to widen participation

Good quality information, advice and guidance is essential to widen participation

Current provision is inadequate

There should be an entitlement to information, advice and guidance about learning opportunities

Summary

To widen participation, potential learners need to be able to get information about available opportunities. They need advice and guidance before, during and at the end of their learning experiences. Current provision is inadequate; it is patchy in its location, in the range of services offered and in its quality. Some initiatives have already been taken to tackle these problems. A national entitlement to information, advice and guidance for all should form part of the national strategy for post-16 learning.

Recommendations

The government should:

- establish a national entitlement to information, advice and guidance as part of its strategy for post-16 learning
- include the entitlement to guidance in the new learners' charter which should replace the charter for further education

- ensure that an entitlement to guidance is included in any proposals to introduce learning accounts

- evaluate the contribution of the new arrangements for the careers service to widening participation.

The Council should:

- include in the guidelines to colleges on self-assessment and inspection a requirement that their guidance services meet the new national standards developed by the Guidance Council.

Advice and Guidance – A Way Through the Maze

Every would-be learner needs access to good quality information, advice and guidance to help them through the maze of learning opportunities. Advice and guidance has an important role to play in getting the 'best fit' between learners and the opportunities available. It is vital that this 'fit' is improved in this country, and that more learners not only take part but succeed. We cannot afford to dash people's hopes by setting them up to fail, and wasting their hard-won motivation; nor can we afford the resources wasted when learners do not complete programmes or fail them. Everyone should be entitled to obtain the help they need to make sound decisions.

The Right to Know

Clear information – in simple straightforward language – must be readily available about the range of opportunities and where each could lead. Information about the time commitment is important. People need to know about the total costs involved and how to finance their learning. For many, information on the availability of childcare and other practical support is essential.

There are many sources of information about learning opportunities. Would-be learners can approach colleges, TECs, careers services, local authorities, voluntary organisations and public libraries. They have to find out where the service is offered, and, usually, make a visit. For some, this in itself constitutes a barrier. We welcome the 'Learning Line', a national telephone helpline due to start in September 1997, which will help to make it easier to find out what is on offer.

Many in the college sector provide drop-in information services and telephone helplines, particularly over the summer months. In colleges, the provision of information is inevitably linked to their promotional efforts. Nevertheless, colleges generally refer enquirers to other providers where they are unable to offer the right course or specialist advice. Many set up stalls in shopping centres and other public places. They find innovative ways of bringing information to the community at enrolment times, such as travelling buses. However, people do not experience a need for information in convenient time-slots, related to annual publicity cycles. They need to be able to gain access to information at the right moment for them, and they need to be aware that it is available. Few colleges can provide the kind of all-year-round service required to meet the potential demand.

Building a Future – The Role of Guidance

Information is only the starting point. It provides the would-be learner with the building blocks for their decision-making. The trick for the individual is how to put the blocks together in the best pattern for them and their future life. It is at this point that advice and guidance can make a critical difference. Good quality advice and guidance, delivered in an impartial way, helps a potential learner make an informed choice. Many new learners underestimate their skills and abilities. Guidance helps them make a realistic assessment of what they can already do, and what they are capable of doing. Specialised careers education and guidance help learners plan their long-term career pathway.

Young people need information on the choices available to them at age 16. Some schools though are unwilling to give their pupils' access to information about the alternatives to sixth form study.[1] The *Education Act 1997* established the right of young people to full information and impartial guidance on the options available at ages 14 and 16. This will be provided in schools by the careers service. We welcome these improved arrangements which recognise young people's 'right to know'. We also welcome the improved entitlements described in the white paper *'Learning to Compete'* which proposed that young people should be guaranteed guidance up to the age of 21 to enable them to enter programmes leading to level 3.[2]

Getting the Most out of Learning

Learners need access to advice and guidance not only before, but during and at the end of their learning programmes. They need help in assessing their progress and in taking action to improve their work. Adults in particular often come to realise their potential once they have started to learn. Success on a basic level course can unleash an ambition to try for a qualification or career which previously would have been considered out of reach. Careful advice and guidance can boost confidence and offer a real chance of success. This kind of guidance may be offered by a professional guidance worker, or by a tutor who has been trained to help students with their personal action-planning.

Advice and guidance forms an essential ingredient of our proposed 'New Learning Pathway'. The 'New Learning Pathway' covers programmes for new learners, comprising a range of units of learning and different ways forward from which choices must be made. Each learner will have to consider their best route through the pathway, and will need advice and guidance both at the start and along the way.

Current Provision is Inadequate

The current provision of advice and guidance is inadequate to support our aim of widening participation. It would be true to say that, at present, anyone who wants initial advice and guidance can generally get it. The snag is that they need to have the self-confidence and awareness of what is available, to seek it out and to present themselves for it. Potential learners, who are outside the magic circle of education and training wherever it is provided, get the worst deal of all.

The provision of information, advice and guidance services is patchy. It is patchy in terms of its geographical location; in terms of the kinds of advice and guidance offered; and in terms of quality. In some areas, TECs have set up effective partnerships through which they collaborate with other providers, including colleges, to provide advice and guidance to agreed standards using trained staff. This way, providers benefit from the sharing of information on educational and training opportunities in the locality, and their clients benefit from quality-assured provision. In other areas, especially rural areas and those with poor transport links, it may be less easy for people to access advice and guidance.

Southall Next Step Centre: effective partnerships in guidance

The Southall Next Step Centre was set up through the partnership of several organisations including the West London TEC, Ealing Tertiary College and the London Borough of Ealing in an area of considerable disadvantage. Next Step is based in a high street location and offers one-to-one careers information and guidance at three levels. There is an open learning centre with access to careers education and guidance reference material, both on paper and computer software. Centre workers are able to speak the majority of community languages and emphasis is put upon providing impartial guidance. We spoke to unemployed business people who were very pleased with the service, particularly the time and trouble taken to listen to them, to discuss their particular needs and to help them prepare their action plans. Many clients progress to courses at the college, or with private training providers.

Existing Further Education Provision

Within the college sector, opportunities are variable. Part-time students, most of whom are adults, receive less educational advice and guidance than full-time and younger students, both before, during and at the end of their courses. Arrangements for careers guidance are also patchy. Some colleges have taken steps to ensure that all students receive the careers guidance they need. In others, careers guidance can be a haphazard affair. Colleges do not give always give sufficient guidance and practical help to students aiming to enter employment. The level of support colleges receive from careers services varies considerably. In some colleges, the amount of time committed by the careers service has been significantly reduced.[3] Few colleges have sufficient trained staff to deliver careers guidance, especially at peak enrolment times.

Good advice and guidance is usually available on the specially-designed courses which provide access to further or higher education for adults. On many other courses, it is a matter of luck whether the course tutor or class teacher is able to spend time with students, discussing their options and possible ways forward. Many teachers will make time to do this, but they may not always have the full information at their disposal. Teachers on non-schedule 2 courses are often an important source of guidance, but they seldom receive training.

The most effective advice and guidance services in colleges are those which operate alongside a range of other support services for students, such as welfare advice and personal counselling. When these services are based on a whole-college policy for student support, which also encompasses personal tutoring, they can have a marked effect in increasing the number of students who stay and complete their courses.

> **Lewisham College: an integrated strategy for information, advice and guidance**
>
> Lewisham College operates in an area of high unemployment and social disadvantage. The average age of its students is 28 years. In this context, the college has developed a strategy to identify and tackle barriers to access and to improve students' completion rates. The college's approach to advice and guidance forms part of this strategy. Advice and guidance services operate alongside a range of other services offering practical support and help with learning. As a result fewer students are dropping out of their courses.

A guidance map has been produced, showing the different types of counselling and guidance – educational, personal, vocational and specialist – and how they are provided before, during and at the end of courses. The guidance team has devised a menu of services for students and staff, described in a leaflet sent to all staff, which helps to de-mystify the services. Guidance workers build relationships with tutors and course team-leaders to provide information and offer support tailored to the needs of students, as necessary, for example in tutor groups. There are close links between the guidance services and local agencies such as the Lewisham refugees' network, and support from the local careers service. There is an information service provided by telephone or for drop-in customers. Pre-entry guidance is offered throughout the year, and there are special services for enquirers with special learning needs, for refugees and asylum-seekers.

Opening up the Magic Circle

It is a matter of luck for people in employment, whether or not they have access to guidance on their training needs. Day-release opportunities have been greatly reduced in recent years. Employee development schemes offer an advice and guidance service to help employees decide on the development opportunities which would suit them best. However, most people in low-paid, unskilled jobs are less likely than their better-educated colleagues to be offered further training by their employer. Only 14 per cent of employers who provide training have a strategy for addressing their employees' basic skills needs.[4] For many employed people an open access guidance service, independent of their employers, would be beneficial.

A special effort is necessary to encourage the most disadvantaged members of society to seek advice and guidance. These may be people who are in part-time or low-skilled jobs, who are unemployed or whose first language is not English. They may have poor educational attainment and no previous family history of benefit from education. Their common characteristic is a lack of confidence in approaching any formal provision which is connected with education or officialdom. Ways need to be found of making contact with these individuals. Some will not have the necessary confidence, or language skills, to use the 'Learning Line'. There are examples of effective local strategies where providers of advice and guidance work directly with community groups and youth clubs. At national level, a concerted publicity campaign is needed which makes use of the popular media.

Ben Jonson Access Centre: networking to meet the needs of the disadvantaged

The Ben Jonson Advice and Guidance Centre in Stepney is one of six drop-in centres in the borough of Tower Hamlets, funded through the Single Regeneration Budget. The centres are located in local shop fronts. They provide a free service, and no time limits are imposed on visits to the centres. A key aspect of the Ben Jonson Centre's work is its networking with local community groups and voluntary organisations. The centre has had to work hard to attract clients. The low self-esteem of local people means they are nervous of approaching official agencies. They are also reluctant to travel outside the borough. This is particularly true of young Asian women. Centre staff have successfully visited groups of women in community venues. They also work with youth groups to make contact with disaffected young people. The Centre offers tuition in English and information technology, a homework club and health and welfare advice for community groups. These activities increase the Centre's profile and encourage more clients to seek advice and guidance on education and training.

Making it Good: Quality Assurance

There is no guarantee at present that advice and guidance will be of good quality. The best quality assurance arrangements exist where providers have collaborated to work to agreed standards, such as in the TEC consortia. Other local partnerships have developed standards specifically for careers education and guidance. Some colleges are members of these groups and are operating quality standards. At national level, much is being done to develop the quality of guidance. National vocational qualifications have been developed for guidance workers. National standards for guidance are being prepared by the Guidance Council. The government has published principles for good practice in careers education, and is preparing a good practice guide on local quality standards in careers guidance. We welcome these developments. They should form the basis of colleges' own quality assurance arrangements. The Council's inspectorate should use the national standards for guidance to provide benchmarks for their judgements about the quality of colleges' guidance provision. On its part, the government should evaluate the contribution to widening participation of the new arrangements for the careers service which have recently been introduced.

New Technology and Guidance

Information technology has the power to transform the information, advice and guidance services of the future. Software already exists for people to identify their skills and interests and cross-relate these to possible careers. Well-designed electronic databases of the learning opportunities which exist within a region are needed, so that all providers of guidance have access to comprehensive information. These databases should be accessible via computer networks so that they can be speedily updated. The proposed 'Learning Information Networks' will develop such databases as part of the local services designed to support the national 'Learning Line'. This will enable callers to the national line to be referred to local advice and guidance services which are supported by good local information.

Interactive databases which give learners the power to assess their needs and provide them with information could be made accessible via the Internet, either in people's homes or in libraries and community venues. Electronic records of achievement, such as the 'UCAS Profile', acting as a database of lifelong learning, are likely to form the basis of individuals' course and career planning. In the long term these or other records could also be used to monitor the take-up of guidance and its effectiveness. Further pilot work is needed to develop these and similar ideas.

An Entitlement for All

We believe that adults should have the same entitlement to advice and guidance as 14 to 21 year olds. Adults should be entitled at least to free initial information and guidance, by telephone, in person, or through a computer link. There should be the option of further in-depth services for which a charge would be made, except for those who are socially or economically disadvantaged. This entitlement should exist regardless of whether a person is currently inside or outside the education system, whether they are in or out of work, and whether or not they are receiving benefits. It should be a lifelong entitlement: people should be able to return for further guidance at any stage of their lives. The 'Learning Line' will offer callers free initial advice and guidance. It will refer them to local services offered through the 'Learning Information Networks' for further help. This is a welcome step forward, but it represents an offer and not an entitlement. Its success for learners will depend on the quality of the local 'Learning Information Networks' and how much of the country they cover.

An entitlement to guidance should be included in a new learners' charter which embraces the concept of lifelong learning. This, in turn, should be linked to the national strategy to stimulate demand in further education. An entitlement to guidance should also be included in any proposals to introduce learning accounts as a strategy for encouraging wider participation.

We believe that guidance services should be firmly rooted in local or regional partnerships, so that they can point learners to real opportunities in the locality. For this reason, we welcome the 'Learning Information Networks'. Local guidance services have great potential as sources of information for local strategic planning of educational provision. They can gather facts about the client group, its needs, aspirations and pathways to success. The strategic partnerships which we propose may not initially comprise the same partners as the 'Learning Information Networks'. They will, however, work within the same context and it will be important that bridges are built between the two from the beginning. Over time, we hope the separate partnerships will come closer and closer together.

Endnotes

1 FEFC and OFSTED, 16–19 Guidance, FEFC, Coventry, 1994

2 DfEE, *Learning to Compete: Education and Training for 14–19 year olds*, CM 3486, The Stationery Office, London, 1966

3 Ibid.

4 DfEE, Basic Skills for Life, DfEE, London, 1997

9 Stimulating the demand for learning

There should be a national publicity campaign to stimulate the demand for learning

Partnership approaches should stimulate demand locally

The power of the media and of new technology must be harnessed to stimulate demand and make learning more accessible

Summary

A national publicity campaign is needed to stimulate the demand for learning. The campaign should make use of the media to convey its message about the value of learning. There should be a 'Charter for Learning' setting out learners' entitlements. The Council should recognise in its aims a responsibility to stimulate demand. The power of television and new technology to deliver accessible and attractive open learning should be fully exploited.

Recommendations

The government should:

- in creating the 'University for Industry', draw upon the expertise of the Council, further education providers and other key organisations, to develop a service which will meet the needs of the widest spectrum of learners, and support the 'New Learning Pathway'

- legislate to make it a duty for all terrestrial television channels to educate as well as to entertain and inform

- work with the BBC and independent broadcasters to explore the possibility of dedicated television channels to support learning

- take steps, in partnership with key national players, to create a mass demand for learning which includes the whole spectrum of the population

- develop a comprehensive 'Charter for Learning', which should be promoted through a national publicity campaign and logo

- make it a key role of the local strategic partnerships to promote clear and consistent messages about the value of learning and the range of opportunities available, and to collaborate with the 'University for Industry' at local level

- develop the role of the Employment Service in promoting the value of, and the opportunities for, learning, particularly to those with little recent experience of learning or who lack basic skills and qualifications.

The Council should:

- recognise in its aims that it has responsibility to work with others to encourage and promote demand for learning

- welcome and promote the potential new role for the further education sector created by the 'University for Industry'.

Changing the Way We See Learning

What is needed is a sea-change in the public attitude to learning. We have seen the evidence of many initiatives to widen participation at local and national levels. All this work is taking place without the benefit of the kind of loud, visible and entertaining publicity campaign which, on a daily basis, persuades the population that it needs all sorts of products, many of which are a lot less useful in the long term than education and training.

A society which is so expert in selling goods should be able to find ways of selling education. The idea of 'learning gain' should be regarded as being just as important for individuals and society as good health and physical fitness. The links between mental and physical fitness should be made and emphasised: the benefits which arise from learning in terms of relaxation, self-esteem, social and family development and economic advancement.

We need to publicise the value of learning nationally, taking advantage of all the means at our disposal. The media – newspapers, magazines, radio and television – have the power to bring the message into every home in the land. They can promote a positive view of learning as a friendly, accessible activity, using images and drama storylines which sell these ideas in a simple way. New technology can transform learning and free it from the constraints of time and place, but only if it is energised in the right way.

Breaking Down the Barriers to Learning

Traditional approaches to attracting learners are not reaching a wide enough spectrum of the population. Promotional activities are successful in recruiting people who are receptive to the idea of learning; people for whom learning holds a promise of benefit. The challenge is to reach the non-learners – people who do not respond to prospectuses, leaflets and advertisements, no matter how well they are produced. These are people who feel that learning is not for them, and who do not seek information.[1]

Reaching Out

There is much exciting and innovative work going on which stimulates wider participation. Many in the further education sector run successful outreach courses, which bring people into education who would not have dreamed of going to main college buildings. There are many voluntary organisations which work with people from under-represented and under-privileged groups, such as those excluded from school and young offenders, and help them to achieve. Outreach and voluntary provision is meeting the needs of some groups in some localities, but it is not on a large enough scale.

Stimulating Demand for Learning in the Workplace

There have been a number of initiatives to stimulate demand for learning in the workplace, many of them funded directly or indirectly by government. Despite all the activity, there remains considerable scope for improving training and educational opportunities for people in work, particularly the unskilled and workers in small and medium-sized firms who are less likely to be offered training.

Working Together to Promote Learning

The strategic partnerships we propose would work together to promote a demand for learning. They would jointly identify under-represented groups in their area and find ways of stimulating demand amongst those groups. The Employment Service, for example, is ideally placed to widen participation in learning among unemployed people and part-time workers. This should involve helping people to find ways of improving basic skills, encouraging manual workers to make positive use of their time out of work to learn and get qualifications.

The partnerships would combine traditional promotional methods with outreach and community work and use of the local media. The partnerships would present a clear and consistent message about the value of learning and the range of opportunities available. This would be mutually beneficial to the partners and would result in a more efficient use of resources. Would-be learners would be encouraged to contact information, advice and guidance services jointly provided by the partners or other local networks. These services, in turn, would help to stimulate demand. They would collect information about clients in the locality, and their needs, to inform future strategic planning.

Harnessing the Power of the Media:
A National Strategy

The massive potential of the popular media to stimulate the demand for learning is largely unexploited. Newspapers, magazines, local and national radio, cable and mainstream television can and do already reach learners. The BBC, in particular, has a long and honourable history of educational broadcasting. But the media's capacity to reach members of the general public, to help them to see learning as something relevant and beneficial to their lives, has yet to be developed in any deliberate and systematic way.

There is strong evidence of the effectiveness of campaigns in the national media. In 1995, some 250,000 people asked for information packs after three 90-second advertisements for the Basic Skills Agency Family Literacy Campaign were shown by the BBC. Co-ordinated national publicity campaigns for education have proved their worth. Adult Learners' Week is an annual event which is co-ordinated nationally by NIACE, the national organisation for adult learners. There are 5,000 local events and broadcasting on all terrestrial, cable and satellite television channels as well as BBC and commercial radio. A free telephone helpline has attracted up to 57,000 callers annually, a third of whom take up courses as a result of the advice, and more than half of whom are long-term unemployed people.[2]

It is time to draw the lessons from these examples, and build upon existing government initiatives to increase the take-up of learning. The government should take the lead in stimulating the demand for learning. The initiative should be ongoing, popular in appeal, draw in all providers, make use of the media and be co-ordinated with local activity. It should harness the enormous potential of the national and local media to reach people in their own homes and workplaces, and to convince people that learning can be relevant and beneficial to their lives. The government should call upon the expertise of media professionals to help it design the best approaches.

A New Charter for Learning

As part of the strategy to stimulate demand, there should be a new 'Charter for Learning'. This would set out the rights of all individual learners aged over 16. It should explain in simple terms what every learner is entitled to in terms of advice and guidance, funding, support, teaching and the quality of education and training.

The launch of the 'Charter' should be part of the national publicity campaign to stimulate demand. It should be co-ordinated with local activities designed to draw people's attention to local advice and guidance services and to the range of courses available. There should be a recognisable logo for the 'Charter' which can be used to identify local activities which promote learning.

Publicity should be generated through advertisements, newspaper and magazine articles and short, dramatised publicity films, all featuring the logo. Television companies should be persuaded to include more positive images of education in their popular soap operas and dramas. Realistic storylines can provide good role models and raise people's awareness that education is for 'ordinary' people, too. For example, the well-liked character Michelle Fowler in *Eastenders* took an access course and went to university. More stories of this kind can help to encourage viewers to take the plunge into education and training.

Technology: A Revolution in Learning

We are moving into a world where the media and information technology will revolutionise access to learning. The danger is that these services, if not harnessed for the benefit of all, will focus their attention on those customers who can pay well: large companies, universities and individuals with credit cards. Terrestrial television companies have already been freed from the obligation to provide educational programming, under the *Broadcasting Act 1990*. This should be reversed as the first step towards building a new relationship between education and the commercial media. Such a reversal would emphasise that organisations which wield as much power as commercial television companies are expected to exercise social responsibility.

The time has come for the combined potential of television and technology to be properly exploited for the benefit of learners in further education. Some colleges have already recognised this. They have developed regional computer networks, so that students in remote locations can have access to interactive open learning materials. One college offers video-conferencing with schools to deliver language teaching. Another has its own cable television station broadcasting four hours a day. Some colleges are collaborating in ambitious 'teleregion' projects with other colleges, universities, local authorities and others. A number of colleges and the National Open College Network have collaborated with the BBC offering viewers the chance to seek accreditation for learning, based on the 'Summer Nights' programmes broadcast by the BBC. The Open University has demonstrated what television can do for learners, when supported by written material and tutoring.

Derwentside College: telematics

The college is running a rural vocational training project jointly with Northumberland TEC and the Rural Development Council, supported by the European Social Fund. People in remote rural areas, who already possess a suitable computer, are provided with a modem to enable them to access distance learning materials. Instruction is given in the use of e-mail. Project participants download learning packages directly to their own computers. There is on-line support through a graphical bulletin board. Tutorial support is also delivered electronically and through use of the telephone, fax and voice mail. The project is already recruiting students from small and medium-size enterprises and from amongst the housebound and disabled.

Advances in technology mean that learners can now access course materials directly through the Internet or local computer networks, no matter where they live, what time of day or year they need to study, or whether they are physically disabled. This has the potential to offer learners more than convenience. Complex concepts can be explained with the help of animation. Learners can interact with the material on the computer, for instance, trying out the effects of different solutions to a problem. They will be able to gain access to libraries of support materials.

The Higginson Committee on learning and technology made a number of detailed recommendations to the Council in 1996.[3] These timely recommendations have since been further developed to prepare the college sector to make the best use of new technology. They include the setting up of projects by colleges to demonstrate particular applications, such as networked course information services or a catalogue of teaching material to be made available on computer networks. The local computer networks developed by colleges and others should be interconnected. A continuing research programme is recommended to examine the effectiveness of new approaches to teaching and learning using new technology. A national staff development programme has been launched to train 50,000 staff in the use of new technologies.

Technology and Adult Learning

Television and computer technology together have the power to revolutionise learning for the twenty first century. They can bring learning to everyone – at home, at college, in workplaces, prisons and outreach centres. We welcome the government's proposals for a 'University for Industry' (UfI). The intention is to improve the availability and quality of learning materials for adults, increasing and widening participation and stimulating demand through new technology.

One of the important areas that UfI will target are people working in small and medium-sized enterprises that, often due to lack resources, undertake little or no training. It could be the hub of a national learning network extending to workplaces, homes and local learning centres. These local centres might include libraries, colleges, schools after hours and community centres. The intention is that UfI will not award its own qualifications. Rather, it will act as a 'cataloguer' and 'broker' of information, materials, courses and services. It will provide access to user-friendly venues on the Internet and create links with tutors and other learners. It will sustain a system of support and guidance services and stimulate mass-marketing of learning opportunities.

The UfI could be the most exciting innovation ever in further education. We want it to reach out to all potential learners, not just those in employment. We want entry points which are not tied too rigidly to particular vocational routes. The media and technology should be used to support general and academic courses for adults, such as English for speakers of other languages and access courses. It may be that the title 'University for Industry' is too specific to cover the range of lifelong learning activities which are needed.

There is great potential for the use of the media and technology in supporting the 'New Learning Pathway'. Television programmes or video recordings could provide illustrated lectures which might be used by individuals at home or in open learning centres, as well as by teachers working with groups. Students working independently could download written text from computers. They could interact with materials on their machines. Tuition, assessment and support could be provided through local colleges and other providers, either in person or electronically. These developments need not kill off the traditional aspects of adult education, such as group work, which have great value in themselves. Rather, they would allow for greater flexibility in the way programmes are delivered.

When developing the UfI, the government should work closely with the Council, further education providers and other key organisations to devise a service which will meet the needs of the widest spectrum of learners and support the 'New Learning Pathway'. Its proposals to exploit the benefits of new technology for learners should build upon the work of the Higginson Committee. The government should work with the BBC and independent broadcasters to explore the possibility of dedicated television channels to support learning.

The Council

The Council has a part to play in creating a culture of innovation and collaborative practice. It should recognise that the motivation of learners is central to widening participation and should recognise in its aims the responsibility to work with others to encourage and promote demand for learning.

Endnotes

1   Individual Commitment to Learning: Understanding Learner Motivation, Crowder and Pupynin of *Minds at Work*, Employment Department, 1995

2   NIACE research for the committee

3   FEFC, *Report of the Learning and Technology Committee*, FEFC, Coventry, 1996

A Widening Participation Committee

Terms of Reference

To identify:

a.   those who do not now participate in further education;

b.   those for whom the quality of participation indicated by completion and achievement rates are less than the norm for the sector;

c.   how participation may be increased and the quality of participation improved;

and to recommend to the Council:

a.   how its strategies, including the funding methodology, should be developed both to increase, and to improve the quality of participation; and the achievement of the national targets;

b.   how information on good practice in institutions in developing and implementing strategies to increase and improve the quality of participation should be disseminated;

c.   how the Council should monitor and evaluate the effect of its strategies;

d.   any further work which needs to be undertaken in relation to increasing and improving the quality of participation.

B Widening Participation Committee

Evidence

The conclusions of the committee are based on a wide range of evidence.

This includes:

- a review of research and literature by the Centre for Economic Performance. This was published as *Widening Participation in Further Education and Training: A Survey of the Issues* in September 1996. Copies were sent to colleges and others funded by the Council. Further copies are available from the Centre for Economic Performance

- a study undertaken by FEDA on the implementation of a credit framework for further education

- a study undertaken by NIACE on stimulating demand for further education among underrepresented groups by collaboration with the media

- a review of research and literature on student financial support in the further education sector and its impact on participation by the Policy Studies Institute

- six evidence sessions from national organisations: National Commission on Education, Association for Colleges, Confederation of British Industry, Further Education Development Agency, Association of County Councils/Association of Metropolitan Authorities, National Union of Students

- the responses to a request for data and other evidence which was published and widely distributed in February 1996.

There were 533 responses to the request from national organisations, colleges, higher education institutions, local authorities, adult education services, training and enterprise councils (TECs), careers services, private training providers, local voluntary organisations and individuals working in further education. The major issues raised were student financial support, funding and the Council's funding methodology, partnership and collaboration, guidance and flexibility of provision

- the responses to the committee's publications *Pathways to Success* and consultation document. There were over 200 responses. There was general support for the initiatives and agreement about the need to target people of 18 years of age and above. A number of helpful suggestions were made and these will be taken account of the development of the 'New Learning Pathway' and in the invitation to apply for funds for the strategic partnerships

- 12 presentations from the Council, Professor John Tomlinson, chairman of the learning difficulties and/or disabilities committee, the Department for Education and Employment, the Further Education Funding Council for Wales, the Further Education Funding Unit of the Scottish Office, the National Institute of Adult and Continuing Education, the Basic Skills Agency, the TEC National Council and the BBC Education Service

- the findings of a seminar of experts with experience of a range of public and private organisations; it debated the impact on widening participation of approaches based on market principles and competition and those which involved partnership and planning

- the findings of a seminar of experts on the development of the 'New Learning Pathway'

- the findings of a seminar on funding issues and options for change; it debated how good practice in widening participation could be reflected in funding arrangements and how under-represented groups could be identified in the current funding arrangements

- visits to colleges and other providers, attendance at national and local conferences and meetings of the Council's regional committees

- analysis of the individualised student record and other data by the staff in the Council's research and statistics team

- specialist research and analysis of inspectorate evidence by the staff of the Council's inspectorate

C Widening Participation Committee

Chairman	Helena Kennedy QC

Members

Pat Brookfield	Former vice-principal, Joseph Chamberlain Sixth Form College
Imtiaz Farookhi	Former chief executive, Leicester City Council, chief executive, National Housebuilding Council
David Eade	Chief executive, Barnsley College (to August 1995)
Richard Guy	Chief executive, Manchester Training and Enterprise Council
Mike Harrison	Vice-chancellor, University of Wolverhampton
Tony Higgins	Chief executive, Universities and Colleges Admissions Service
Ted Parker	Principal, Barking College
Alison Scott	Principal, Somerset College of Arts and Technology
Maggie Semple	Director of education and training, The Arts Council of England
Anne Sofer	Former director of education and community services, Tower Hamlets
Judith Summers	Chair, executive committee, National Institute of Adult Continuing Education
George Sweeney	Principal, Knowsley Community College (from September 1995)
Ann Tanner	Managing director, Tanner Foods Ltd (to February 1997)

Co-opted Members

Pam Gibson — Head of customer and community services, Kent County Council

Barfuor Adjei -Barwuah — Education staff, Further Education Development Agency

Anna Reisenberger — Head of programme, participation and achievement, Further Education Development Agency

Assessors

Valerie Bayliss — Department for Education and Employment (to November 1995)

Felicity Everiss — Department for Education and Employment (from January 1996)

Stephen Kershaw — Department for Education and Employment

Observers

Elaine Allinson — Further Education Funding Council for Wales (to December 1996)

Ann Jenkins — Further Education Funding Council for Wales (from January 1997)

Joyce Johnston — Further Education Funding Division, The Scottish Office (to September 1996)

Maureen McGinn — Further Education Funding Division, The Scottish Office (from October 1996)